The Popcorn Lover's Book

Sue Spitler &
Nao Hauser

Contemporary Books, Inc.
Chicago

Library of Congress Cataloging in Publication Data

Spitler, Sue.
The popcorn lover's book.

Includes index.
1. Cookery (Popcorn)   I. Hauser, Nao.   II. Title.
TX814.5.P66S64   1983   641.6'5677   83-5230
ISBN 0-8092-5542-1

Copyright © 1983 by Sue Spitler and Nao Hauser
All rights reserved
Published by Contemporary Books, Inc.
180 North Michigan Avenue, Chicago, Illinois 60601
Manufactured in the United States of America
Library of Congress Catalog Card Number: 83-5230
International Standard Book Number: 0-8092-5542-1

Published simultaneously in Canada by
Beaverbooks, Ltd.
150 Lesmill Road
Don Mills, Ontario M3B 2T5
Canada

Contents

Acknowledgments

For their dedication to popcorn, and their generous help, we would like to thank Dr. Bruce Ashman of Purdue University, Patricia Belth of the Peekskill Area Health Center, D. J. Bennett, Wayne and Milly Blewitt of Consolidated Popcorn Inc., George K. Brown of the Wyandot Popcorn Co., Pam Leeming of the Wyandot Popcorn Museum, Charles Cretors and Lynn Maurer of C. Cretors & Company, Garry Smith of the American Pop Corn Company, Ginny Blair and Melanie Jones of The Popcorn Institute, and Kathleen E. German, our tireless tester and taster.

Chapter 1

The Art of Popping Corn

If you've ever measured an evening's hours by the bowlful . . . if you've ever listened for the *sound* of your favorite snack . . . if you've ever stopped beneath a movie marquee just to sniff the popcorn inside . . . then you qualify for membership in the popcorn lovers' club.

Memories make you eligible, too. If you recall the crunch of your first movie date . . . if Saturday nights once meant "Perry Mason" and popcorn . . . if you raced your brothers and sisters to the bottom of the bowl . . . if the circus bleachers were strewn with crushed kernels . . . if you can still feel moist caramel in the palm of your hand . . . if the happy ending made you cry, and you reached for the popcorn so no one would see. . . .

The only immutable requirements are popping corn and a way to make it pop. If you're still using the blackened pressure cooker you got as a wedding present (without the pressure gauge, of course), that's fine. If you swear by premeasured packets of corn and oil, or pop-in-the-package tin foil balloons, that's fine, too. True popcorn lovers know that popcorn is a state of solace. How you get there doesn't matter.

Since World War II, however, developments in the popcorn industry have increased opportunities for connoisseurship. The

1

corn you buy nowadays is not the same corn that made *King Kong* (1933) memorable at the movies or "Mr. Peepers" (1952–55) unforgettable at home. (And it's a far cry, indeed, from the Aztec popcorn headdresses that stole the show when Cortez greeted the Mexican natives in 1519.) Today's corn pops to greater volume than ever before, and it shouldn't leave a mess of unpopped "old maids" lying in the bottom of the popper. It is also probably yellow on the outside, although forty years ago, it more likely would have been white—and a thousand years ago it could have been blue, red, purple, or black.

The product facts are these:

- The best popping corn, according to Dr. Bruce Ashman, leader of the popcorn development program at Purdue University, now yields forty-three to forty-four cubic centimeters of popcorn per gram—approximately 22 percent more than it did in the mid-1950s. Since 1936, volume expansion has almost doubled.
- Some hybrid kernels pop bigger than others. Popcorn packers who sell to consumers tend to call this product "gourmet." Packers who sell to concessionaires call it "theater-style," meaning that it takes fewer kernels to fill the containers moviegoers pay for.
- It isn't necessarily the movie, the man in your life, or the smell of your best girl's hair that suddenly makes the popcorn taste better than ever. It could be the vintage. Some years' harvests simply yield better-tasting popcorn than others. As with wine, the weather is a major, unpredictable determinant of quality.

- It doesn't pay to stockpile vintage popcorn. Chances are it will dry out. Popcorn pops because there is moisture inside each kernel (ideally, 13 to 15 percent); when heated, the moisture turns into steam power. If the popcorn dries out, it runs out of steam. If you didn't know this, but you have noticed that your choice packages just don't pop the way they did months or years ago, there's still hope. The Popcorn Institute recommends that you fill a one-quart jar three-fourths full with popcorn and add one tablespoon of water. Cover the jar and shake it frequently, about every five or ten minutes, until all the water has been absorbed. In two to four days, the popcorn should revive.
- You can expect that about 97 percent of the kernels you purchase fresh will pop, according to the Popcorn Institute. To preserve popability, store popcorn in an airtight container and refrigerate it.

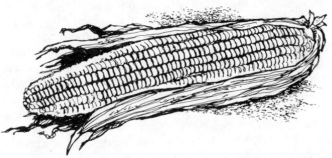

- If you like white-hulled popcorn, chances are you live in the Midwest—and chances are that's the only place you'll find it. Until 1935, white popping corn dominated the market; now it accounts for less than 5 percent of sales, most of which are in the Corn Belt. White popcorn usually doesn't expand as much as yellow-hulled kernels. Some connoisseurs love it; others find it tasteless.
- There is no such thing as hull-less popcorn. The closest thing you'll find in the supermarket is a puffed corn meal product that resembles popped kernels—but it's not real popcorn. If you want to tenderize real popped corn, spread it on baking sheets and place it in a 250-degree oven for several hours. The popped corn will become tenderer as the moisture evaporates.

- Some stores sell popcorn on the cob as a novelty item. Yes, you can pop it on the cob—but it tastes tough and terrible. Once you've shelled a cob or two, you'll appreciate the reason why virtually all popcorn sold today has been mechanically shelled. In recent years, most popcorn farmers have acquired combines that harvest and shell the corn simultaneously. (Orville Redenbacher may be the last holdout against this innovation—the corn that bears his name is still picked and stored on the ear, although it is mechanically shelled prior to packaging. Owned by Hunt-Wesson Foods, Orville Redenbacher's Gourmet Popping Corn is the nation's top-selling brand.)
- One type of popcorn you will not find in stores is the tougher breed preferred by processors who make cheese corn, caramel corn, and other popcorn snacks. They buy corn that will not easily break when the popped kernels are mechanically mixed with seasonings or coatings. For caramel corn, they particularly like a type of popcorn that pops into mushroom-shaped kernels—the better to coat evenly with the caramel syrup. Because you're able to treat corn more gently than a machine can, you can use regular, naturally tender popcorn for all homemade snacks and confections.
- If you happen across some red or blue popcorn at a country farm stand or other out-of-the-way outlet, be assured that it will yield the same white popped kernels as yellow- or white-hulled varieties.
- Sweet corn is a close relative of popcorn, but it will not pop. Don't even think about trying it. Use popped *popcorn* when recipes call for popped corn.
- The best thing that ever happened to popcorn, according to one old-time popcorn processor we know, was the Food and Drug Administration, which enforces rigid standards of popcorn storage sanitation, thus ensuring that the product you buy now is a whole sight cleaner than much of the stuff shipped fifty years ago.

Our own history of corn-popping implements only goes back as far as the scorched pot that served our interests between episodes of "Danny Thomas" and "December Bride." They tell us there were other tools around before then. Native Americans were known to hold ears of popcorn over an open fire on sticks. Sometimes they covered hot embers with sand and popcorn and waited for the kernels to pop out. Later they invented covered clay pots with handles, some of which are now displayed at the Field Museum of Natural History in Chicago and other museums. European settlers crafted perforated sheet-iron poppers and attached handles long enough to keep hands at a safe distance from the fire. Gas ranges began to ease the cook's burden in the late nineteenth century. The earliest electric poppers entered households in the 1920s—usually as an optional attachment that could be plugged into the newfangled electric stove.

POPCORN POW WOW

North American Indians sorting ears of popcorn and sifting popped corn with reed sieve. Clay popcorn popper shown in foreground. Illustration courtesy of Wyandot Popcorn Museum.

Currently available options include these:

- A three- or four-quart aluminum or stainless steel covered saucepan. It will work best if you first heat a thin layer of vegetable oil (about ¼ cup) and add a few kernels of popcorn; when the trial kernels begin to pop, pour a single layer of popcorn into the pot. Cover and shake gently from time to time as the kernels pop. Don't wait for the pop of the last diehard kernel before removing the pot from the heat—you're likely to scorch the whole batch for the sake of one kernel. You can pop corn in a pot without oil, but you have to keep the pot in motion to prevent the corn from scorching. Either way, the test kernels should pop in 1½ to 2 minutes. If they take longer, your stove setting is probably too low— medium-high is about right. If they pop faster, reduce the stove temperature. Corn popped too slow or too fast will be tough. Some steam should escape from the pot as the corn pops; so the pot lid should not fit too tightly.

• An electric popper. These freestanding machines have advanced the cause of TV attentiveness by making it possible to pop corn right in the living room or den. Moreover, their performance is more predictable than the vicissitudes of pot-shaking. You can choose a model that pops the corn in oil or one that pops it in nothing more than a burst of hot air. Calorie-watchers may prefer the latter method. Other popcorn lovers have complained that the absence of oil diminishes the flavor. For the sake of safety and effectiveness, we recommend that you select a model that carries the Popcorn Institute Seal of Quality Performance. For a list of these, you can write to the Popcorn Institute, 111 East Wacker Drive, Chicago, Illinois 60601.

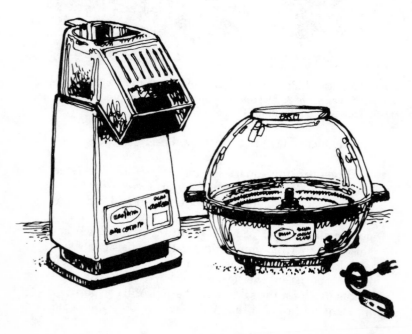

- A microwave popcorn popper. If your microwave oven owner's manual recommends popping corn in the oven, you may enjoy the speed and convenience offered by one of the specially designed microwave poppers. All of these will pop corn without oil; some have an oil-use option. Do not pop corn in a paper bag or microwave casserole; the dangers include fire and breakage. If you don't have a microwave popper, you might want to try one of the special pop-in-the-container microwave popcorn brands; however, these products may be too highly salted and seasoned for your taste. Be aware that microwave popping usually results in more unpopped kernels than other methods, especially if the moisture content of the popcorn is low. Please note that the Microwave Methods you'll find in this book apply only to already popped corn. Whichever way you choose to pop the popcorn, you may wish to take advantage of microwave speed and convenience for the other cooking steps.
- Heavy-duty aluminum foil and a barbecue grill. This is the latter-day version of campfire popcorn. For each serving, place one teaspoon of oil and one tablespoon of popcorn on a 12-inch square of foil. Bring the corners of each square together and twist them loosely to seal. Place the packets on the grill and listen for the popping to start and stop. This method can bring popcorn closer to the stars or to the mosquitoes on a summer night, depending on your point of view.

The mechanics of popcorn are important, but it's the sensation that really counts. Some people like to enhance the sensation by popping the corn in naturally flavorful coconut oil or in specially formulated butter-flavored popping oil, although any plain vegetable oil is suitable for popping. Melted butter and bacon drippings should not be used for popping since they tend to burn; these seasonings, like salt, should only be drizzled over already-popped corn. For a very delicate, sweet flavor, you might try this trick: Pop corn as usual, using cooking oil. Just as the corn begins to pop, sprinkle one tablespoon of sugar over the kernels. Cover the pot or popper quickly and continue popping.

The recipes in this book call for plain popped popcorn. You can pop the corn any way you wish. One tablespoon of unpopped corn will yield approximately one quart of popped corn. Our formulas include seasoned butters, seasoned salts, and beverages to serve with popcorn, as well as many varieties of caramel corn, cheese corn, and other favorites. You'll also find a few surprises—both highly munchable and of the dream-making kind.

Chapter 2

Well-Seasoned Popcorn

Popcorn and the movies first met by chance at the 1893 Columbian Exposition, the Chicago World's Fair that ushered in the age of electricity. At one of the exhibition halls, Thomas A. Edison demonstrated his prototype movie projector. Outside, amidst the 633 acres of fairgrounds, Charles Cretors, a baker by trade, drew crowds to another revolutionary invention—his gasoline-fired automatic corn popper.

Not long afterward, the movie projector became established in nickelodeons across the country. People paid a nickel apiece to roar with laughter at the Keystone Cops and open their hearts to Mary Pickford. They nourished fun and fantasies with popcorn—but it was scooped from a Cretors wagon parked down the block, for the theater owners wanted no part of the noisy vendors or their trade.

Although it now seems like a marriage made in heaven, the popcorn–movie courtship was an uphill struggle. Charles Cretors paved the way for greater intimacy when he invented the electric popper, in 1916. This machine, and subsequent refinements, made commercial indoor popping safer. But even then, proprietors of most of the increasingly posh theaters feared sullying their grand lobbies with a sideshow of popcorn. The

An ornate Cretors Wagon attracts popcorn lovers, circa 1895.

Great Depression of the 1930s scared them into viewing things differently. By the mid-thirties, theater owners looked forward to "reaping the harvest of nickels" from popcorn on their own premises—and the once-familiar sight of sidewalk salesmen, pushing, and later driving, wagons around town, began to fade from the scene.

Everyone who has ever settled into wide-screen darkness with a warm container of crunchy kernels has his or her own tale of popcorn and movies to tell. . . .

For us, it started at a drive-in in 1955. The movie was *The Seven Little Foys*, with Bob Hope and James Cagney. But the main feature, to our way of thinking, was a big advertisement flashed on the screen before the show began. It showed nothing but two cardboard containers of butter-drizzled popcorn, while an announcement blared through the car hookup speaker, ". . . at the snack bar now!" And though the muggy air on that summer night was at least a hundred degrees, the only thing we longed to dive into was the jumbo family size.

By concessionaire standards, we were the perfect audience. A 1953 article in *The Popcorn Merchandiser*, a trade journal for vendors, lauded buttered popcorn as "a new toy for us to play with, a very profitable idea." The kernel of the idea, of course, was that a golden shower of butter would inevitably tempt moviegoers to pay more for the corn. And lest the screen-oglers end up with puddles of butter in their laps, an auxiliary product was promoted at the same time—sturdy waxed containers to replace the old-fashioned cardboard boxes and paper bags.

Mary Pickford in DOROTHY VERNON OF HADDON HALL.

Photo courtesy of *Wide World Photos*.

Surrendering hours at the movies to greasy-fingered dreams, we remained ignorant of the business end of things. They tell us now that the reason the popcorn tasted so good had nothing to do with Tab Hunter or Natalie Wood. They suggest it was the anhydrous butter—a specially processed curdless butter that remains melted at room temperature, long after the popcorn may have cooled. While it may be true that the butter (or, sometimes, butter-flavored oil) dispensed from the squirter pump was a purer form of fat than the butter we buy, we doubt that it accounted for our lust. After all, the popcorn clutched in our greedy hands never had a chance to cool off.

When we were young, the movies first let us spy on grown-up romance and then gave us big-date destinations. Nowadays, we need neither diversion, and we'd just as soon eat the popcorn at home. Not only is the munching cheaper, but we get to set the stage for, and star in, our own reveries. And we can season the butter, if not the dialogue, with intrigue and suspense.

What goes well with melted butter? Well, a dash of imagination, of course. But, more to the point, ingredients that evoke the urbanity of Cary Grant, the cheerfulness of Doris Day, the fascination of Marlon Brando, the cosmopolitanism of Sophia Loren . . . and that can also be readily reached for whenever a snack is needed. These recipes fit the billing. Each will season six to eight cups of popped corn.

For best coverage, drizzle half of the seasoned butter over half of the popcorn and stir; then repeat with the other half. You can add salt, if you wish, after stirring each half. If you want to reduce caloric intake, spread the same amount of butter or margarine over more popcorn; if you use diet margarine, you'll need to melt almost twice as much to match the proportions of other ingredients.

The mixtures that follow can be refrigerated or frozen just like plain butters. You may wish to make double or triple batches, chill them until they are firm enough to handle, and shape them into sticks; that way you can conveniently cut off pats of seasoned butter and melt them anytime. You'll find that these recipes are just as delicious melted over vegetables and grilled or broiled meats as they are with popcorn.

Herbed Mustard Butter

   3 to 4 tablespoons butter or margarine
   1 tablespoon Dijon-style mustard

1 teaspoon soy sauce
¼ teaspoon dried rosemary leaves
¼ teaspoon lemon juice

Melt butter in small saucepan; stir in mustard, soy sauce, rosemary, and lemon juice. *Makes about ¼ cup.*

Cheddar Tomato Butter

3 to 4 tablespoons butter or margarine
2 teaspoons instant tomato soup mix
2 teaspoons powdered Cheddar cheese sauce mix
½ teaspoon dried basil leaves
⅛ teaspoon pepper

Melt butter in small saucepan; stir in tomato soup mix, Cheddar cheese sauce mix, basil, and pepper. *Makes about ¼ cup.*

Note: *Soup and sauce mixes can be found in the sections of supermarkets where dried mixes and salad dressings are displayed.*

Chutney Butter

3 to 4 tablespoons butter or margarine
3 tablespoons minced chutney

Heat butter and chutney in small saucepan until butter is melted. *Makes about ⅓ cup.*

Cardamom Butter

3 to 4 tablespoons butter or margarine
½ teaspoon granulated sugar
½ teaspoon ground cardamom
¼ teaspoon ground allspice

Melt butter in small saucepan; stir in sugar, cardamom, and allspice. *Makes about ¼ cup.*

Note: *This recipe is excellent with popcorn popped with sugar (see page 8).*

Chili Butter

3 to 4 tablespoons butter or margarine
1   teaspoon chili powder
½ teaspoon ground cumin
2   teaspoons dried sour cream sauce mix

Melt butter in small saucepan; stir in chili powder, cumin, and dried sour cream sauce mix. *Makes about ¼ cup.*

Note: *Dried sour cream sauce mix can be found in the sections of supermarkets where dried mixes and salad dressings are displayed.*

Pesto Butter

3 to 4 tablespoons butter or margarine
¼ cup grated Parmesan cheese
1½ teaspoons dried basil leaves
½ teaspoon garlic powder

Melt butter in small saucepan; stir in cheese, basil, and garlic powder. *Makes about ⅓ cup.*

Note: *Italian pesto sauce usually is made with pine nuts or walnuts, as well as basil, Parmesan cheese, and garlic. So you may wish to mix the popcorn with some toasted nuts before adding Pesto Butter.*

Fruit Butter

3 to 4 tablespoons butter or margarine
1   tablespoon apricot or peach preserves
½ teaspoon lemon juice

Melt butter in small saucepan; stir in preserves and lemon juice. *Makes about ¼ cup.*

After years of wallowing in the buttery stuff, we discovered the joys of plain, salted popcorn. The change came over us in a wave of devotion to old, late-night movies. We'd like to be able to boast that loyalty to Edward G. Robinson in *Little Caesar* (1930) and Humphrey Bogart in *Casablanca* (1942) turned us into tougher characters—capable, at least, of resisting butterfat. But it wasn't that way at all. If anything, it was the weightless magic of Fred Astaire and the wispy waistline of Lauren Bacall that inspired our low-calorie conversion.

Photo courtesy of **Wide World Photos.**

Fred Astaire in HOLIDAY INN.

Many old-timers claim that butter was a transgression in the first place—that it masks the naturally rich flavor of popcorn. We wouldn't go that far. But we'll gladly take our popcorn straight up if there's a shaker of seasoned salt at hand. You can sprinkle the following mixtures onto buttered or unbuttered kernels. But do keep a stock in a convenient shaker—one of those inexpensive tin flour dusters serves the purpose well— and make extra supplies for popcorn-loving friends at holiday gift time. You'll find that a good shake of any of these mixtures will also enliven vegetables, meats, egg noodles, casseroles, and many other foods. Fill several shakers with various salts and you'll have both a good seasoning selection for all-purpose cooking and the makings of an instant popcorn party.

By starting with coarse salt and blending it to a fine powder in these recipes, you'll achieve perfect popcorn-sprinkling texture. Both kosher and sea salt are appropriate types of coarse salt. Be sure that the cover is securely on your blender before you turn the machine on—or you're likely to shower the whole room with seasonings. If you need to restrict salt intake, you can omit the salt and use only the herb blends for seasoning, but they will not adhere well unless the popcorn is lightly buttered. You can also grind a salt substitute with the herbs, if you wish.

Herbed Salt

¼ cup coarse salt
1 teaspoon dried basil leaves
1 teaspoon dried marjoram leaves
½ teaspoon dried thyme leaves
½ teaspoon dried onion flakes

Process all ingredients in blender at high speed until mixture is very fine in texture, 30 to 45 seconds. *Makes about ¼ cup.*

Texas Salt

¼ cup coarse salt
2 teaspoons chili powder
1 teaspoon ground cumin
½ teaspoon garlic powder
½ teaspoon dried onion flakes
¼ teaspoon cayenne pepper

Process all ingredients in blender at high speed until mixture is very fine in texture, 30 to 45 seconds. *Makes about ¼ cup.*

Dill Salt

¼ cup coarse salt
2 teaspoons dried dillweed

1   **teaspoon dried chives**
1   **teaspoon dried parsley flakes**
½   **teaspoon garlic powder**

Process all ingredients in blender at high speed until mixture is very fine in texture, 30 to 45 seconds. *Makes about ¼ cup.*

Caraway Salt

¼   **cup coarse salt**
2   **tablespoons caraway seeds**
1   **teaspoon dry mustard**

Process all ingredients in blender at high speed until mixture is very fine in texture, 30 to 45 seconds. *Makes about ⅓ cup.*

Sesame Salt

2   **tablespoons coarse salt**
2   **tablespoons toasted sesame seeds**
¼   **teaspoon ground turmeric**

Process all ingredients in blender at high speed until mixture is very fine in texture, 30 to 45 seconds. *Makes about ¼ cup.*

According to movie concessionaires, one of the blessings of having two hands is that you can hold a carton of popcorn in one and a soft drink in the other. Indeed, popcorn merchandising experts caution vendors against selling popcorn in bags, since it is difficult to balance these while munching and sipping simultaneously. You can solve the juggling problem at home, of course, by serving the popcorn in a bowl. But that won't do anything to quench your thirst. So we offer here a half dozen beverages created to match the various moods of popcorn.

You might invite friends over for Bourbon Sours and popcorn the next time *Gone with the Wind* is scheduled on TV. We like to reach for Sunrise Punch during the late-night scenes of *Casablanca* or *It Happened One Night*. Wine Coolers are appropriate whenever the hero is 1930s-suave or the heroine Diorishly dressed. The mellowness of Spiced Coffee Cream suits a cold winter's eve with Bing Crosby. And we guarantee that the best way to cap off the Marx Brothers' antics is with Top Banana Shakes.

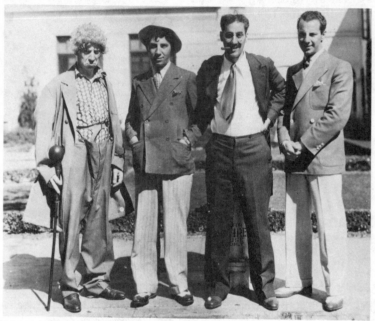

The Four Marx Brothers.   Photo courtesy of Wide World Photos.

Bourbon Sours

Juice of 2 oranges (1 to 1¼ cups)
Juice of 2 lemons (⅓ to ½ cup)
½ cup bourbon whiskey
3 tablespoons granulated sugar
2 egg whites
Ice cubes
4 orange slices

Process orange juice, lemon juice, bourbon, sugar, and egg whites in blender at high speed until foamy; pour over ice in glasses. Garnish with orange slices. *Makes 4 servings (about 4 ounces each).*

Bullfighters' Cocktails

    1 can (24 ounces) vegetable juice cocktail, chilled
    2 cups beef bouillon, chilled
    1 tablespoon lemon juice
    1 tablespoon lime juice
    2 teaspoons Worcestershire sauce
    1 teaspoon prepared horseradish
    2 dashes red pepper sauce
    ½ teaspoon celery salt
    Ice cubes
    Lime wedges

Mix vegetable juice, bouillon, lemon juice, lime juice, Worcestershire sauce, horseradish, red pepper sauce, and celery salt; pour
over ice in tall glasses. Garnish with lime wedges. *Makes 8 servings (about 5 ounces each).*

Note: *If desired, stir ¾ to 1 cup chilled vodka into mixture before serving.*

Sunrise Punch

    1 can (12 ounces) frozen lemonade concentrate
    1 package (10 ounces) frozen unsweetened
        strawberries, partially thawed
    2 cups water
    1 can (6 ounces) frozen mixed fruit concentrate,
        thawed
    2 cups chilled lemon-lime soda
    Ice cubes
    Lemon slices

Process lemonade concentrate, strawberries, and water in
blender at high speed until smooth; pour into punch bowl or
pitcher. Stir in mixed fruit concentrate, lemon-lime soda, and
ice cubes. Garnish with lemon slices. *Makes 12 servings (about 5
ounces each).*

Note: *If desired, stir 1 to 1½ cups chilled rum or vodka into punch before
serving.*

Wine Coolers

1 cup water
¼ cup granulated sugar
Rind of ½ orange
Rind of ¼ lemon
2 cups dry red wine, chilled
1 cup lemon-lime soda, chilled
Ice cubes
Orange slices

Heat water, sugar, orange rind, and lemon rind to boiling in small saucepan, stirring until sugar is dissolved. Reduce heat and simmer 15 minutes; cool to room temperature. Strain mixture; discard rind. Refrigerate until chilled.

Mix wine, sugar syrup, and lemon-lime soda in pitcher; pour over ice in tall glasses. Garnish with orange slices. *Makes 4 servings (about 6 ounces each).*

Spiced Coffee Cream

4 cups strong coffee
⅓ cup granulated sugar
8 whole allspice
8 whole cloves
2 cinnamon sticks
1½ cups vanilla ice cream
Ground nutmeg

Heat coffee, sugar, allspice, cloves, and cinnamon sticks to boiling in small saucepan; reduce heat and simmer 15 minutes. Cool to room temperature; strain coffee mixture and discard spices. Refrigerate until chilled.

Pour coffee mixture into 6 tall glasses or mugs; top each with scoop of ice cream, stirring slightly. Sprinkle with nutmeg. *Makes 6 servings (about 8 ounces each).*

Note: *If desired, pour coffee mixture into 6 tall glasses; top with ice cream as above. Fill glasses with chilled club soda. Makes 6 servings (about 10 ounces each).*

Top Banana Shakes

 2 cups chocolate milk
 1 large banana, cut into pieces
 2 tablespoons strawberry preserves
 4 scoops chocolate ice cream (about 2 cups)

Process chocolate milk, banana, and preserves in blender until smooth. Add ice cream; process just until mixed. Pour into tall glasses; serve with straws. *Makes 4 servings (about 8 ounces each).*

Chapter 3

Satisfying
Snack Mixes

Between 1950 and 1963, more than 50 million TV sets entered American homes. News reports linked to early stages of this invasion included these:

- In pre-TV times, 63 percent of all Americans went to sleep well before midnight. But by 1951, surveys showed that more than three-fourths of those with TVs stayed up till the wee hours with Jerry Lester and Dagmar, Steve Allen, and Jack Paar.
- In city after city, movie attendance dropped 20 to 40 percent in 1951, as TV hookups penetrated the hinterlands. By the end of the 1950s, the movies had lost half of their audience. Jukebox receipts, library book checkouts, and taxi fares also dropped.
- On January 19, 1953, millions more Americans tuned in to "I Love Lucy" for the birth of Little Ricky than stayed tuned the following day for the inauguration of President Eisenhower.
- In 1954, seeking fast relief from an Abbott and Costello skit on "The Colgate Comedy Hour," Frank Walsh, of West Hempstead, Long Island, pulled out a gun and shot his TV set. The publicity accorded the slapstick victim

Lucille Ball (left) and Vivian Vance. Photo Courtesy of Wide World Photos.

gained him an invitation to appear on the quiz show
"Strike It Rich"—where he won a brand-new TV the
following week.

- By 1956, Americans were spending more hours watching TV than they were at work. Televisions were selling
at the rate of twenty thousand a day.
- By 1963, popcorn sales had risen more than 70 percent
from a decade earlier.

It was not coincidence but foresight that prompted business-
man Ben Banowitz to create a popcorn product called "TV
Time" around 1950. By 1952, the tie between TV and popcorn
sales was already so well evident that the popcorn industry
chose as the theme of its annual convention, "Popcorn—
America's Newest Big Business."

If you have a very good memory for TV trivia, you may
remember the episode of "Mama" in which Dagmar (played by
Robin Morgan) outdid a rival schoolmate by inviting the whole
class over for big bowls of popcorn—an inspiration provided by
Mama (Peggy Wood), of course. We invite you to outdistance all
other TV-watching snacks with the bonanza bowlful at the top
of the next page.

All-American Snack Mix

6 cups popped popcorn
2 cups pretzel sticks
1½ cups French-fried onion rings
1 cup canned shoestring potatoes
1 cup spoon-size shredded wheat cereal
1 cup cocktail peanuts
4 to 6 slices bacon, fried, crumbled
6 tablespoons butter or margarine
1 tablespoon Worcestershire sauce
⅛ teaspoon red pepper sauce

Combine popped corn, pretzel sticks, onion rings, potatoes, cereal, peanuts, and bacon in large bowl. Melt butter in small saucepan; stir in Worcestershire sauce and red pepper sauce. Pour over popped corn mixture and toss. *Makes about 11 cups.*

If you grew up with TV in the late fifties, chances are you remember Ward Bond, Wyatt Earp, and Matt Dillon. Paladin may still be your model of coolness, Bat Masterson your image of style. From 1957 to 1960, the Wild West ruled the ratings, capturing seven out of ten of the top places. We salute the era with this appropriate mix of corn power and gumption.

James Arness (left), Dennis Weaver (center), and Amanda Blake (right) in "Gunsmoke." Photo Courtesy of Wide World Photos.

Texas Snack Mix

- 3 cups corn chips
- 3 cups Corn Chex cereal
- ¼ cup butter or margarine
- 1 tablespoon crushed dried red pepper
- 2 teaspoons Worcestershire sauce
- 2 teaspoons chili powder
- ⅛ teaspoon garlic powder
- 6 cups popped popcorn

Combine corn chips and cereal in jelly roll pan. Melt butter in small saucepan; stir in dried red pepper, Worcestershire sauce, chili powder, and garlic powder. Pour half the butter mixture over the corn chip mixture and toss. Pour remaining butter mixture over popped corn in large bowl; toss. Bake corn chip mixture at 300°F. for 30 minutes, stirring in popped corn during last 15 minutes. *Makes about 12 cups.*

> **Microwave Method:** Microwave butter in 6-quart glass bowl at High until melted. Stir in remaining ingredients, adding popped corn last. Microwave at High until crisp, 6 to 8 minutes, stirring every 2 minutes.

You don't need a drop of nostalgia to appreciate the mix of caramel and cheese corn that follows at the top of the next page. But if you ever whiled away half-hours with the saccharine wisdom of "Leave It to Beaver," "Father Knows Best," and "The Donna Reed Show," you'll recognize that this is the recipe equivalent of what used to be called a "warm family" sitcom—very engaging and mildly addictive!

Sweet and Savory Popcorn

- 3 tablespoons light corn syrup
- 2 tablespoons half-and-half
- ¼ cup butter or margarine
- ½ cup packed light brown sugar
- 10 cups popped popcorn
- 3 tablespoons butter or margarine
- 3 tablespoons grated American cheese

Heat corn syrup, half-and-half, ¼ cup butter, and the sugar to boiling in medium saucepan, stirring until sugar is dissolved; boil 2 minutes. Pour sugar mixture over 4 cups of the popped corn in medium bowl, stirring to coat evenly. Spread popped corn mixture in jelly roll pan. Bake at 300°F. for 30 to 35 minutes. Cool to room temperature; break into pieces.

Melt 3 tablespoons butter in small saucepan; stir in grated cheese. Pour butter mixture over remaining 6 cups popped corn in large bowl; toss. Add caramel corn; toss. *Makes about 10 cups.*

Note: *Grated American cheese usually can be found beside the grated Parmesan cheese in supermarkets.*

Microwave Method: Microwave corn syrup, half-and-half, ¼ cup butter, and the sugar in 2-quart glass casserole at High 2 minutes; stir. Microwave at 70% for 2 minutes. Pour mixture over 4 cups of the popped corn in 3-quart glass casserole. Microwave at High 4 minutes, stirring every minute. Cool in jelly roll pan.

Microwave 3 tablespoons butter in small glass bowl at High until melted; stir in grated cheese. Proceed as above.

Nowadays, we crave something more nourishing than "Bewitched" and "Gilligan's Island." Or, more to the point, at our age we want to look like we know what we're gobbling up.

The following three mixtures, two savory and one sweet, demonstrate the point. The first will make even the most sophisticated viewer reach for the cheese corn, the second stands up completely to "antijunk" snobs, and the third satisfies a hunger for sweets with both panache and vitamins.

Two-Cheese Popcorn

¼ **cup butter or margarine**
1 **ounce blue cheese, crumbled**
10 **cups popped popcorn**
¼ **cup grated Parmesan cheese**

Melt butter in small saucepan; stir in blue cheese until melted. Pour butter mixture over popped corn in large bowl; toss. Sprinkle with Parmesan cheese and toss. *Makes about 10 cups.*

Mixed Vegetable Popcorn

¾ cup dried mushrooms
¼ cup dried sweet pepper flakes
2 tablespoons dried chopped onion
6 tablespoons butter or margarine
10 cups popped popcorn

Sauté mushrooms, pepper flakes, and onion in butter in medium skillet until mushrooms soften, about 3 minutes.

Spoon vegetable mixture over popped corn in large bowl and toss. *Makes about 10 cups.*

Apricot Corn Crunch

4 cups popped corn
2 cups Rice Chex cereal
1 cup mixed nuts
½ cup dried banana chips
½ cup chopped dried apricots
¼ cup butter or margarine
2 tablespoons apricot preserves
2 tablespoons light brown sugar

Combine popped corn, cereal, nuts, banana chips, and apricots in large bowl. Melt butter in small saucepan; stir in preserves and sugar until melted. Pour butter mixture over popped corn mixture and toss. Spread popped corn mixture in jelly roll pan; bake at 350°F. for 10 minutes. *Makes about 7 cups.*

Microwave Method: Microwave butter in glass baking dish, 13″ × 9″ × 2″, at High until melted. Stir in preserves and sugar; stir in remaining ingredients. Microwave at High 6 minutes, stirring every minute.

It has been said that TV brought the world into our living rooms. It can also be said that in the last twenty years or so, we have brought both TV and popcorn to the world. Almost all of the global popcorn crop is grown in the United States, and one-tenth of it is shipped abroad. Nigeria, Japan, Saudi Arabia, Italy, and Spain are among the top customers. Sweden is fast approaching America's annual popcorn munching rate of more than forty quarts per capita. Even the French, known for their pâté predilections, are beginning to eat popcorn—although not as avidly as they consume installments of "Dallas."

Having spent much of our lives foraging for snacks at thirty-minute intervals—whether the breaks came between reruns of "My Little Margie" and "Love That Bob" or scenes from "Masterpiece Theatre"—we have found that the best refreshment comes when we broaden our own popcorn horizons. The results are chronicled in this travelogue of snack mixes. It starts most aptly in Mexico, where Aztecs were popping corn thousands of years ago. It includes a stop in India for a fabulous curry and a detour to China for a noodle-crunched mix. Most likely to make conversation are Popcorn Provençal, a play on the famous flavors of the south of France, and Indonesian Snack Mix, which features the irresistible eye appeal of puffed shrimp chips.

Mexican Snack Mix

> 4 cups tortilla chips
> 1 cup cocktail peanuts
> ¼ cup butter or margarine
> 2 tablespoons dried sour cream sauce mix
> 1 tablespoon dried chives
> 1 teaspoon chili powder
> 1 teaspoon ground cumin
> ¼ teaspoon garlic powder
> ¼ teaspoon red pepper sauce
> 6 cups popped popcorn

Combine tortilla chips and peanuts in jelly roll pan. Melt butter in small saucepan; stir in dried sour cream sauce mix, chives, chili powder, cumin, garlic powder, and red pepper sauce.

Pour half the butter mixture over tortilla chip mixture and toss. Pour remaining butter mixture over popped corn in large bowl and toss. Bake tortilla chip mixture at 300°F. for 30 minutes, stirring in popped corn during last 15 minutes. *Makes about 10 cups.*

Note: *Dried sour cream sauce mix can be found in the sections of supermarkets where dried mixes and salad dressings are displayed.*

Microwave Method: Microwave butter in 6-quart glass bowl at High until melted. Stir in remaining ingredients, adding popped corn last. Microwave at High until crisp, 6 to 8 minutes, stirring every 2 minutes.

Italian Snack Mix

  2 ounces sliced pepperoni, cut into strips
  ¼ cup butter or margarine
  2 teaspoons dried basil leaves
  1 teaspoon dried oregano leaves
  ½ teaspoon dried thyme leaves
  ¼ teaspoon garlic powder
  8 cups popped popcorn
  ½ cup toasted pine nuts or slivered almonds
  ⅓ cup grated Parmesan cheese

Sauté pepperoni in small skillet until crisp; drain on paper toweling. Melt butter in skillet; stir in basil, oregano, thyme, and garlic powder. Pour butter mixture over popped corn in large bowl and toss. Add pepperoni, nuts, and cheese, and toss. *Makes about 8 cups.*

Popcorn Provençal

  ½ cup butter or margarine, softened
  1½ teaspoons garlic powder
  ½ teaspoon dried basil leaves
  ¼ teaspoon dried tarragon leaves
  6 slices French bread (scant ½ inch thick)
  ½ can (16-ounce size) pitted ripe olives, drained, cut
     into strips
  1 to 2 anchovy fillets, mashed
  8 cups popped popcorn

Mix butter, garlic powder, basil, and tarragon in small bowl; spread 3 tablespoons of the butter mixture on both sides of bread slices. Cut bread slices into scant ½-inch cubes; sauté in large skillet until golden. Remove from skillet.

  Melt 1 tablespoon of the butter mixture in skillet; sauté olives until crisp. Add remaining butter mixture and the anchovies; cook over medium heat until melted. Pour mixture over popped corn and toss. *Makes about 10 cups.*

Note: *If desired, 3 cups dried unseasoned croutons can be substituted for the homemade croutons. Sauté croutons with 3 tablespoons of the butter mixture until golden; complete recipe as above.*

Bavarian Snack Mix

    4 slices pumpernickel bread
    Butter or margarine
    6 cups popped popcorn
    2 cups pretzel sticks
    ¼ cup butter or margarine
    1 tablespoon spicy brown mustard
    1 teaspoon caraway seeds, crushed
    ½ teaspoon dried dillweed

Spread both sides of bread slices lightly with butter; cut bread into scant ½-inch cubes. Sauté bread cubes in medium skillet until crisp. Combine bread cubes, popped corn, and pretzel sticks in large bowl. Melt ¼ cup butter in skillet; stir in mustard, caraway seeds, and dillweed. Pour butter mixture over popped corn mixture and toss. *Makes about 10 cups.*

Greek Islands Snack Mix

    6 tablespoons butter or margarine
    1 teaspoon dried oregano leaves
    ½ teaspoon ground cinnamon
    ¼ teaspoon garlic powder
    Rind of 1 lemon, grated
    10 cups popped popcorn
    2 ounces feta cheese, well drained, crumbled

Melt butter in small saucepan; stir in oregano, cinnamon, garlic powder, and lemon rind. Pour over popped corn in large bowl and toss. Sprinkle with cheese and toss. *Makes about 10 cups.*

Curried Corn Mix

- 2 cups Wheat Chex cereal
- 2 cups Rice Chex cereal
- 1 cup cashews
- 1 cup flaked coconut
- ½ cup finely chopped onion
- ½ cup butter or margarine
- 2 teaspoons curry powder
- ¹⁄₁₆ teaspoon cayenne pepper
- 4 cups popped popcorn
- 1 cup dark raisins

Combine cereal, cashews, and coconut in large bowl. Sauté onion in butter in small skillet until tender, about 4 minutes; stir in curry and cayenne. Pour butter mixture over cereal mixture and toss to coat evenly. Spread mixture in ungreased jelly roll pan. Bake at 250°F. for 45 minutes, stirring every 15 minutes. Stir in popped corn and raisins during last 15 minutes. *Makes about 10 cups.*

Microwave Method: Microwave butter in glass baking dish, 13″ × 9″ × 2″, at High until melted. Stir in remaining ingredients except raisins. Microwave at High until crisp, 7 to 8 minutes, stirring every 2 minutes. Stir in raisins for last 2 minutes of microwave time.

Indonesian Snack Mix

- 2 ounces imitation shrimp-flavored chips
- Vegetable oil
- ½ cup cocktail peanuts or slivered almonds
- 3 tablespoons butter or margarine
- 2 teaspoons soy sauce
- ¼ teaspoon ground ginger
- 6 cups popped popcorn
- 1 cup coconut chips or flaked coconut, toasted

Fry shrimp-flavored chips in oil according to package directions; drain on paper toweling. Sauté peanuts in butter in small skillet until golden; stir in soy sauce and ginger. Pour butter mixture over popped corn in large bowl and toss. Add shrimp-flavored chips and coconut and toss. *Makes about 8 cups.*

Note: *Shrimp-flavored chips are available in Oriental markets or in specialty sections of supermarkets. There is no substitute; if not available, omit from recipe.*

Oriental Popcorn Mix

6 **cups popped popcorn**
1 **can (5 ounces) chow mein noodles**
1 **cup cashews**
3 **tablespoons butter or margarine**
1 **tablespoon soy sauce**
½ **teaspoon 5-spice powder**

Combine popped corn, chow mein noodles, and cashews in large bowl. Melt butter in small saucepan; stir in soy sauce and 5-spice powder. Pour butter mixture over popped corn mixture and toss. *Makes about 9 cups.*

Note: *Five-spice powder is available in Oriental markets or in specialty sections of supermarkets. There is no substitute; if not available, omit from recipe.*

To enhance the Oriental flavor of this recipe, you may want to substitute sesame oil for vegetable oil when you pop the corn; the sesame oil gives the popped popcorn a slightly nutty taste that goes well with the soy sauce and 5-spice powder.

Chapter 4

Caramel Corn and Other Confections

While Thomas Edison was winding the reel on his movie projector and Charles Cretors was making corn pop in a steam-powered wagon, F. W. Reuchheim was wooing fairgoers at the 1893 Columbian Exposition with an already popular mix of caramelized corn and peanuts. At that time the confection had no name, and there were no miniature prizes buried in the barrels and tins from which it was sold. Yet Reuchheim knew his product was a winner, because people kept coming back for more.

In 1896, as the story is told, a salesman stuck a label on the mixture by exclaiming, "That's a crackerjack!" Reuchheim seized the word and added to it his diet-decimating slogan, "The More You Eat, the More You Want." Soon afterwards, he started packing the product in waxed paper-lined boxes, which made national distribution possible.

Competitive caramel-corn makers—the sweetness of their products marred, perhaps, by sour grapes—now like to claim that Cracker Jack wasn't nearly as good as other mixtures around at the time. It was the packaging, they say, that gave Reuchheim's corn an edge by keeping it fresh and crisp.

In truth, there were many caramel-corn peddlers around be-

Cracker Jack was first introduced in 1872 by F. W. Reuchheim, whose product was an instant success with fairgoers at the 1893 World's Fair. By 1948, Cracker Jack was distributed in almost every nation in the world.

fore the turn of the century. The product may have been more popular than plain popcorn, since it was, as Cracker Jack spokesmen have always insisted, a confection, and not just a snack. Evidence of Cracker Jack's appeal to children came in 1908, when a songwriter, unconnected to the company, put the plea for peanuts and Cracker Jack into "Take Me Out to the Ballgame." Four years later, youngsters won a bonus when Cracker Jack began packing a prize in each box. After World War I, Sailor Jack and his dog Bingo took up permanent residence on the package. By 1948, Cracker Jack was distributed in almost every nation in the world—and with it some twenty million prizes each month.

Although we have long considered "The More You Eat, the More You Want," to exemplify truth in advertising, the part of the Cracker Jack story that has really stuck is the way F. W. Reuchheim got started. In 1872, all he had was $200, a single corn popper, and a recipe. But demand was so great that he was forced to expand production facilities five times between 1875 and 1884. The 1893 World's Fair was his first attempt to introduce the product to a wider-than-regional audience. And the rest, as they say, is history. Today, Cracker Jack, now owned by the Borden Company, utilizes the nation's single largest popcorn popping plant.

Ever since we learned about Reuchheim, we've been searching for the flavor combination that might put a little "history" into our bank accounts. So far, the hottest prospect we've found is the following mouth-watering blend of popcorn, chopped nuts, coffee, and cocoa.

Mocha Caramel Corn

- 8 **cups popped popcorn**
- 1 **cup toasted chopped hazelnuts or blanched almonds**
- 1 **cup packed light brown sugar**
- ½ **cup very strong coffee**
- ½ **cup light corn syrup**
- ¼ **cup butter or margarine**
- 2 **tablespoons cocoa**

Combine popped corn and hazelnuts in large bowl. Heat sugar, coffee, corn syrup, butter, and cocoa to boiling in small saucepan, stirring until sugar is dissolved. Reduce heat to low; cook, stirring occasionally, until mixture reaches 270°F. on candy thermometer. Pour syrup mixture over popped corn mixture, stirring to coat evenly. Cool to room temperature; break into pieces. *Makes about 1¼ pounds.*

Microwave Method: Microwave sugar, coffee, corn syrup, butter, and cocoa in 2-quart glass casserole at High 3 minutes, stirring after 1½ minutes. Microwave at 70% until mixture reaches 270°F. on candy thermometer, 6 to 7 minutes. Proceed as above.

Another contender we're considering is the Kentucky Derby winner at the top of the next page. Bourbon, peanuts, and sesame—or "benne," as it's called down South—give it a definite regional accent. But the crunch and the corn should bring it coast-to-coast coverage.

Kentucky Derby Caramel Corn

6 cups popped popcorn
1 cup cocktail peanuts
1 cup sesame sticks
1 cup granulated sugar
½ cup dark corn syrup
⅓ cup bourbon whiskey
¼ cup butter or margarine

Combine popped corn, peanuts, and sesame sticks in large bowl. Heat sugar, corn syrup, bourbon, and butter to boiling in medium saucepan, stirring until sugar is dissolved. Reduce heat to low; cook, stirring occasionally, until mixture reaches 270°F. on candy thermometer. Pour syrup mixture over popped corn mixture, stirring to coat evenly. Cool to room temperature; break into pieces. *Makes about 1 pound.*

> **Microwave Method:** Microwave sugar, corn syrup, bourbon, and butter in 2-quart glass casserole at High 2 minutes; stir. Microwave at 70% until mixture reaches 270°F. on candy thermometer, 6 to 7 minutes. Proceed as above.

Glamour is the secret ingredient of California Combo—in the highly seductive form of pistachios, sunflower nuts, and a subtle orange fragrance. The formula's whipping cream is the catalyst for a slightly more crackly crunch—somewhat like a candy apple.

California Combo

6 cups popped popcorn
1 cup pistachio nuts or slivered almonds
½ cup sunflower nuts
½ cup light corn syrup
¼ cup frozen orange juice concentrate, thawed
2 tablespoons whipping cream or half-and-half
¾ cup packed light brown sugar
3 tablespoons butter or margarine
1 tablespoon grated orange rind

Combine popped corn, pistachios, and sunflower nuts in large bowl. Heat corn syrup, orange juice concentrate, cream, sugar, and butter to boiling in medium saucepan, stirring until sugar is dissolved. Reduce heat to low; cook, stirring occasionally, until mixture reaches 260°F. on candy thermometer. Stir in orange rind. Pour syrup mixture over popped corn mixture, stirring to coat evenly. Cool to room temperature; break into pieces. *Makes about 1 pound.*

> **Microwave Method:** Microwave corn syrup, orange juice concentrate, cream, sugar, and butter in 2-quart glass casserole at High 2 minutes; stir. Microwave at 70% until mixture reaches 260°F. on candy thermometer, 6 to 7 minutes. Proceed as above.

For the homiest fireside setting, Apple Pumpkin Spice Crunch is the mixture we'd choose. Not only is it absolutely delicious, but it takes us back to the scene of the earliest American colonists, whose standard party provisions were popcorn, apples, and cider.

Apple Pumpkin Spice Crunch

   6 cups popped popcorn
   1 cup coarsely chopped dried apples
   ¾ cup toasted chopped walnuts
   ¼ cup light molasses
   ¼ cup light corn syrup
   2 tablespoons butter or margarine
   2 tablespoons light brown sugar
   2 tablespoons granulated sugar
   ½ teaspoon pumpkin pie spice

Combine popped corn, apples, and walnuts in large bowl. Heat molasses, corn syrup, butter, brown sugar, granulated sugar, and pumpkin pie spice to boiling in small saucepan, stirring until sugar is dissolved. Reduce heat to low; cook, stirring occasionally, until mixture reaches 285°F. on candy thermometer. Pour syrup mixture over popped corn mixture, stirring to coat evenly. Cool to room temperature; break into pieces. *Makes about 1 pound.*

No doubt you've noticed that all of our caramel corn recipes so far have called for a candy thermometer. This tool is not absolutely necessary, but it is your best assurance that the caramel will cool to the right consistency—neither too hard nor too sticky. If you don't have a candy thermometer, you can test the syrup by dropping a bit from a teaspoon into cold water and rolling it between your fingers; if it forms a hard ball, it's ready to pour over the corn. You may have to test a few times before it's right—and you're likely to conclude that it would have been a lot easier to use a thermometer. Be careful not to let the thermometer touch the bottom of the pan or the reading will not be accurate. If you are following Microwave Methods, use a specially made microwave candy thermometer or remove the syrup from the oven before testing it with a conventional candy thermometer; do not leave a conventional thermometer in the microwave oven.

Once we saw copper caldrons bubbling with syrup—and inhaled the most memorable fragrance—on the premises of a commercial caramel corn manufacturer, Popped-Right of Marion, Ohio. We noticed that there wasn't a single candy thermometer to be found. "We gauge doneness just by the color—and by the steam that rises when the syrup mixture reaches 280 to 285 degrees," the quality manager told us. But we don't recommend that you follow his lead at home—the caramel will get much too hard. Despite their homespun methodology, the Popped-Right people have their own secrets (only viable on a commercial scale) for turning out a perfect product. If you nevertheless resist the thought of using a candy thermometer, you can still make an excellent caramel corn by baking the corn in the syrup. This method will yield a lighter caramel corn, and the kernels will remain easily separable. Because the concept translates especially well to microwave oven techniques, we also include here a fabulous formula for Microwave Caramel Corn.

Baked Caramel Corn

6 tablespoons light corn syrup
¼ cup half-and-half
½ cup butter or margarine
1 cup packed light brown sugar
8 cups popped popcorn

Heat corn syrup, half-and-half, butter, and sugar to boiling in medium saucepan, stirring until sugar is dissolved; boil 2 minutes. Pour sugar mixture over popped corn in large bowl, stirring to coat evenly. Spread corn in jelly roll pan. Bake at 300°F. for 30 to 35 minutes. Cool to room temperature; break into pieces. *Makes about 8 cups.*

Island Caramel Corn

   8 cups popped popcorn
   1 cup flaked coconut, toasted
   ⅓ cup chopped pitted dates
   ⅓ cup chopped candied pineapple
   ½ cup butter or margarine
   ⅓ cup dark corn syrup
   ¼ cup canned cream of coconut
   1 cup packed dark brown sugar

   Combine popped corn, coconut, dates, and pineapple in jelly roll pan. Heat butter, corn syrup, cream of coconut, and sugar to boiling in medium saucepan; boil 2 minutes. Pour syrup mixture over popped corn mixture, stirring to coat evenly. Bake at 300°F. for 30 to 35 minutes. Cool to room temperature; break into pieces. *Makes about 8 cups.*

   Microwave Method: Microwave butter, corn syrup, cream of coconut, and sugar in 2-quart glass casserole at High 2 minutes; stir. Microwave at 70% for 4 minutes, stirring after 2 minutes. Pour over popped corn mixture in 6-quart glass bowl, stirring to coat evenly. Microwave at High until crisp, 5 to 6 minutes, stirring every minute. Spread in jelly roll pan to cool.

Microwave Caramel Corn

   16 cups popped popcorn
   ½ cup butter or margarine
   ¼ cup dark corn syrup
   1 cup packed light brown sugar
   1 teaspoon vanilla
   ½ teaspoon baking soda

Place popped corn in large, heavy, brown paper grocery bag. Microwave butter, corn syrup, and sugar in 8-cup glass measure, uncovered, at High 5 minutes, stirring every 2 minutes. Stir in vanilla and baking soda. Pour syrup mixture over popped corn in bag; close bag, folding top of bag down twice to close securely. Shake well. Microwave at High 2 minutes, shaking bag every minute. Microwave at High 30 seconds; shake bag and pour mixture into serving bowl; let cool. *Makes about 16 cups.*

Note: *The paper bag ensures that each grain of popped corn will be evenly coated with the caramel. If you prefer, you can divide the popped corn between 2 heatproof 3-quart glass bowls. Make syrup mixture as above and pour half the mixture into each bowl; toss well. Microwave 1 bowl at a time, as above, stirring every minute. Do not pop the corn in a paper bag.*

Butter is the key ingredient of caramel corn. Remove the butter, lower the temperature of the syrup, and the popcorn becomes lightly candied rather than caramelized. The kernels remain white—and the scent of star anise in the following recipe complements well their delicacy.

Anise Candied Popcorn

> 8 cups popped popcorn
> 1 cup toasted slivered almonds
> 1¼ cups granulated sugar
> ⅔ cup water
> ¼ cup light corn syrup
> 6 to 8 star anise

Combine popped corn and almonds in large bowl. Heat sugar, water, corn syrup, and anise to boiling in medium saucepan, stirring until sugar is dissolved. Reduce heat to low; cook, stirring occasionally, until mixture reaches 250°F. on candy thermometer. Discard star anise. Pour syrup mixture over popped corn mixture, stirring to coat evenly. Cool to room temperature. *Makes about 1¼ pounds.*

> **Microwave Method:** Microwave sugar, water, corn syrup, and anise in 2-quart glass casserole at High 2 minutes; stir. Microwave at 70% until mixture reaches 250°F. on candy thermometer, 5 to 6 minutes. Proceed as above.

The next two recipes are very definitely candies, and not caramel corn variations. The syrup for the Almond Popcorn

Brittle is cooked to a stage where it will harden, like the more familiar peanut brittle, as the mixture cools. Popcorn Pralines, although cooked to a lower temperature, acquire the texture of New Orleans's finest from the proportion of liquid to sugar. Both are as worthy of gift wrapping as they are of self-indulgence.

Almond Popcorn Brittle

½ cup butter or margarine
1 cup granulated sugar
½ cup light corn syrup
¼ cup water
4 cups popped popcorn
1 cup blanched whole almonds

Melt butter in medium saucepan; stir in sugar, corn syrup, and water. Heat to boiling, stirring until sugar is dissolved.

Reduce heat to low; cook, without stirring, until mixture reaches 270°F. on candy thermometer. Remove from heat; stir in popped corn and almonds. Pour into greased jelly roll pan; let cool to room temperature. Break into pieces. *Makes about 1 pound.*

Microwave Method: Microwave butter, sugar, corn syrup, and water in 2-quart glass bowl at High 2 minutes; stir. Microwave at 70% until mixture reaches 270°F. on candy thermometer, 8 to 10 minutes, stirring every 2 minutes. Proceed as above.

Popcorn Pralines

2½ cups granulated sugar
1 cup packed light brown sugar
½ cup whipping cream or half-and-half
½ cup water
¼ cup butter or margarine
¼ teaspoon salt
2 cups popped popcorn
2 cups pecan halves

Combine granulated sugar, brown sugar, cream, water, butter, and salt in large saucepan; heat to boiling, stirring until sugar is dissolved. Reduce heat to low; cook, without stirring, until mixture reaches 234°F. on candy thermometer. Add popped corn and pecans, stirring until mixture is glossy.

Drop mixture by tablespoonfuls onto greased cookie sheets; cool to room temperature. *Makes about 2 dozen.*

Note: *Praline mixture hardens easily. To soften, stir over low heat or keep mixture in top of double boiler over simmering water.*

All popcorn lovers with divided loyalties—divided, that is, between popcorn and chocolate—will want to mix up a batch of Popcorn Nut Fudge without any further ado. It is the easiest confection imaginable and a great counterpoint of creaminess and crunch.

Popcorn Nut Fudge

    4 cups popped popcorn
    1 cup mixed nuts
    1 can (14 ounces) sweetened condensed milk
    3 packages (6 ounces each) semisweet chocolate
       morsels
    2 tablespoons butter or margarine
    1 teaspoon vanilla

Combine popped corn and nuts in aluminum foil-lined 9-inch square baking pan. Combine condensed milk, chocolate morsels, and butter in large saucepan; cook over medium heat until chocolate is melted and mixture is smooth. Stir in vanilla. Pour chocolate mixture over popped corn mixture in baking pan. Refrigerate until set; cut into squares. *Makes about 1½ pounds.*

Microwave Method: Microwave condensed milk, chocolate morsels, and butter in 2-quart glass casserole at 70% until morsels are melted, 6 to 8 minutes, stirring every 2 minutes. Proceed as above.

If you like pecan pie, you'll love Popcorn-Peanut Pie—a circus-inspired dessert that forms its own top crust of popcorn as it bakes. It's easy enough for children to make (with an older person nearby to watch the oven), but adults will compete for a slice—especially with a dollop of whipped cream.

Popcorn-Peanut Pie

1 cup cocktail peanuts
1 unbaked pastry for 9-inch pie
3 cups popped popcorn
2 cups packed light brown sugar
½ cup half-and-half
¼ cup all-purpose flour
1 teaspoon vanilla
3 eggs

Sprinkle peanuts in bottom of pastry; sprinkle popped corn over peanuts. Mix sugar, half-and-half, flour, and vanilla in medium bowl; beat in eggs. Pour sugar mixture into pastry, making sure all the popped corn is coated. Bake at 325°F. until set, about 1¼ hours. Serve slightly warm. *Makes 8 servings.*

Every September the town of Valparaiso, Indiana—Orville Redenbacher's native ground—celebrates popcorn with a parade, contests, and plenty of munching. At festival time, everyone heads over to Browns Ice Cream Parlor for a double scoop of popcorn ice cream. Toffee-flavored and flecked with crushed popcorn, Brazil nuts, and puffed rice cereal, the creamy mixture aims to deliver the best of all possible worlds. You can enjoy similar sensations with these two ice cream–popcorn creations. The ice cream sandwiches are simple servings of a novel pleasure; the pie presents the same contrasting textures in a party mode.

Popcorn Ice Cream Sandwiches

¼ cup butter or margarine
2 tablespoons cherry preserves
2 tablespoons light brown sugar
4 cups popped popcorn
1½ cups vanilla ice cream, slightly softened
Chocolate ice cream topping

Melt butter in small saucepan; stir in preserves and sugar. Pour mixture over popped corn and toss; spread popped corn mixture in baking pan, 13" × 9" × 2". Bake at 350°F. for 10 minutes.

Divide mixture in half; press evenly in bottoms of 2 aluminum foil-lined loaf pans, 9" × 5" × 4". Cool to room temperature.

Spread ice cream evenly over popped corn mixture in 1 pan; top with mixture from second pan, pressing gently into ice cream. Freeze until firm, 8 hours or overnight.

Invert frozen mixture onto serving plate. Cut into slices with serrated knife. Serve with chocolate topping. *Makes 8 servings.*

Microwave Method: Microwave butter, preserves, and sugar in glass baking dish, 13" × 9" × 2", at High until butter is melted; stir. Stir in popped corn; microwave at High 4 minutes, stirring every minute. Proceed as above.

Scoop-of-Popcorn Pie

½ cup whipping cream or half-and-half
¼ cup light corn syrup
¼ cup butter or margarine
1 cup packed light brown sugar
1 teaspoon vanilla
⅛ teaspoon salt
6 cups popped popcorn
1 to 1½ quarts ice cream, any flavor
Assorted ice cream toppings (optional)

Heat cream, corn syrup, butter, sugar, vanilla, and salt to boiling in medium saucepan, stirring until sugar is dissolved. Reduce heat to low; cook, stirring occasionally, until mixture reaches 250°F. on candy thermometer. Pour syrup mixture over popped corn in large bowl, stirring to coat evenly. Cool until warm; press on bottom and sides of greased 9-inch pie pan.

At serving time, fill pie shell with scoops of ice cream. Cut into wedges; serve immediately with selection of toppings. *Makes 8 servings.*

Chapter 5

Popcorn at Every Meal

Fifty-six hundred years ago, New Mexican cave dwellers popped corn to make it edible. No mere sport of snackers back then, popping was the only sure way to soften the rock-hard kernels. The corn was multicolored and tiny—each ear only a fraction of an inch long. An ancestor of both the popcorn and the sweet corn we know today, it came to be known throughout the Americas as *maiz*, which meant "universal mother of that which sustains life."

Centuries later, after softer breeds of corn had evolved, Mexicans renamed popcorn *maiz reventador*, or "exploding corn," to distinguish it from its more docile cousin. They continued to count on it as a dietary staple well into modern times. After grinding tools were developed, corn connoisseurs ground the popped kernels to a fine powder called "pinole." Sometimes flavored with sugar and anise or cinnamon, the cereal prepared from pinole rivaled tortillas as a foodstuff in the region around Guadalajara.

The earliest European settlers in the New World caught on quickly to native ways. In the early 1600s, French explorers shared bowls of popcorn soup with Iroquois tribesmen around the Great Lakes. New England colonists served popcorn with sugar and cream for breakfast.

As the United States grew and prospered, wheat and oats pushed popcorn off the breakfast table. Popcorn went into a severe decline, even as a snack food, until the movies underlined its entertainment value. However, the puffed kernels did enjoy one last burst of glory as a source of nutrition. This came right after World War II, when shortages of wheat and rye flours forced the federal government to ration bakers' supplies. In Chicago, the H. Piper Company responded with bread, muffins, and doughnuts baked from a blend of 75 percent wheat and 25 percent popcorn flour. The company took pride in its ingenuity. First it had to set up and operate its own milling equipment, since other millers refused to grind the hard kernels of un-popped corn. Then it had to come up with a solution to the bread's unfortunate tendency to fall flat from the heaviness of the popcorn flour; this is accomplished by subjecting the ground corn to a special high heat treatment. Rewarded by instant sales success, the Piper Company promised to continue baking pop-corn bread even after wheat supplies were restored. But as far as we know, nary a crumb of the stuff has been seen for more than thirty years.

What we would like to do is revive popcorn's rightful place in everyday nutrition. After all, popcorn comes with the proper credentials: five grams of complex carbohydrate and one gram of protein, as well as calcium, iron, niacin, and riboflavin, in every cupful. If you pop it plain, large-flaked popcorn (the kind most of us buy nowadays) contains twenty-five calories a cup; popped with oil, it contains forty calories.

As the first step in our campaign to legitimize popcorn at mealtimes, we propose that every popcorn lover pull out a plate and a fork. Not only will these serving implements glorify the corn, but they will enable you to indulge in these two full-protein popcorn entrées.

Popcorn on a Plate

    6 cups popped popcorn
    ½ cup chopped green pepper
    4 ounces chopped salami or summer sausage
    6 ounces shredded Swiss cheese
    ⅛ teaspoon ground nutmeg
    ⅛ teaspoon white pepper

Arrange popped corn, green pepper, and salami evenly in bottom of baking pan, 13" × 9" × 2". Sprinkle with cheese; sprinkle with nutmeg and pepper. Bake at 375°F. until cheese is melted, about 5 minutes. Spoon mixture onto plates; serve with forks. *Makes 4 servings.*

Note: *To make Swiss Popcorn Fondue, omit the green pepper and salami; proceed as above.*

Popcorn Nachos

Tortilla chips
1½ cups shredded Monterey Jack cheese
4 cups popped popcorn
½ cup finely chopped cooked chicken breast
2 tablespoons finely chopped, seeded, fresh or
   canned jalapeño peppers
2 tablespoons picante sauce

Arrange single layer of tortilla chips in bottom of 10-inch quiche pan; sprinkle with ½ cup of the cheese. Sprinkle popped corn evenly over cheese; sprinkle with ½ cup cheese.

Combine chicken, jalapeño peppers, and picante sauce; sprinkle over cheese. Sprinkle with remaining ½ cup cheese. Bake at 500°F. until cheese is melted, 3 to 5 minutes. Serve hot. *Makes 4 to 6 servings.*

Note: *Be careful not to touch your eyes when handling jalapeño peppers, as the juice may cause irritation.*

Because popcorn is a whole grain, it satisfies the dietary need for fiber and retains minerals and vitamins that are milled out of refined flours. Therefore, popcorn makes a fine substitute for bread. It is difficult, however, to layer sandwich fillings between kernels. So we've resolved lunchtime logistics in the following recipe by tossing all ingredients in a paper bag.

Submarine Sandwich in a Bag

> 2 ounces sliced ham, cut into thin strips
> 2 ounces sliced salami, cut into thin strips
> 2 ounces sliced pepperoni, cut into thin strips
> 3 tablespoons butter or margarine
> ½ teaspoon dried oregano leaves
> ½ teaspoon crushed dried red pepper
> 4 cups popped popcorn
> 1 cup unseasoned croutons
> 1 tablespoon grated Parmesan cheese

Sauté ham, salami, and pepperoni in 1 tablespoon of the butter in small skillet until crisp; stir in remaining butter, the oregano, and dried red pepper. Pour butter mixture over popped corn and croutons in paper bag; shake to mix. Add cheese; shake to mix. *Makes 4 servings.*

Although popcorn's roots have been traced to the New World, anthropologists long ago noted that primitive communities in Sumatra, northern Burma, and south China grew popcorn and used it in ceremonies of ancient origin. They're still puzzled by how popcorn crossed the Pacific. We'll stake our guess on Chinese Takeout Popcorn—a diet-wise mixture that quells cravings for real Chinese food with the meaty texture of dried Chinese mushrooms and the slightly sweet scent of Szechwan peppercorns. You might pack a sack for your next exploration of bike trails, park, or beach.

Chinese Takeout Popcorn

> 10 medium dried Chinese mushrooms
> 1½ ounces dried beef, cut into thin strips

¼ cup butter or margarine
1 tablespoon dried minced onion
½ teaspoon Szechwan peppercorns, toasted, crushed
6 cups popped popcorn

Coarsely chop mushrooms, discarding stems. Sauté mushrooms and dried beef in 2 tablespoons of the butter until crisp, about 3 minutes. Stir in remaining butter, the onion, and peppercorns. Pour mushroom mixture over popped corn in paper bag; shake to mix. *Makes about 6 cups.*

Note: *Szechwan peppercorns are available in Oriental markets or in specialty sections of supermarkets.*

Compared to the following wake-up mix, the colonial breakfast of sugared popcorn and cream must have been a somewhat soggy affair. We don't recommend downing this granola with cream or milk, but do suggest you grab a handful or two of its quick energy, protein, and iron when there's only time for breakfast-on-the-go.

Popcorn Granola

2 cups quick-cooking oats
1 cup unsalted peanuts
1 cup flaked coconut
¼ cup butter or margarine
½ cup honey
3 tablespoons light brown sugar
1 teaspoon ground cinnamon
4 cups popped popcorn
1 cup golden raisins
½ cup sunflower nuts

Combine oats, peanuts, and coconut in jelly roll pan. Melt butter in small saucepan; stir in 3 tablespoons of the honey, the sugar, and cinnamon; pour over oats mixture and toss. Bake at 300°F. for 30 minutes, stirring every 15 minutes. Stir in popped corn, raisins, and sunflower nuts. Drizzle with remaining honey and stir to coat evenly. Bake 15 minutes longer. *Makes about 8 cups.*

Microwave Method: Microwave butter in glass baking dish, 13" × 9" × 2", at High until melted. Stir in honey, sugar, cinnamon, oats, peanuts, and coconut. Microwave at High 6 minutes, stirring after 3 minutes. Stir in popped corn; microwave at High until crisp, about 7 minutes, stirring every 2 minutes. Stir in raisins and sunflower nuts for last 2 minutes of microwave time.

The sustenance derived by the Iroquois from popcorn soup inspired these combinations of popcorn croutons and soup. Neither is anything like the Indian gruel, of course, and we can no doubt be grateful for that!

Carrot Soup with Parmesan Popcorn Croutons

½ cup chopped onion
2 tablespoons butter or margarine
2 cups sliced carrots
1 cup cubed pared potato
3 cups chicken broth
¼ cup whipping cream or half-and-half
¼ cup plain yogurt
½ teaspoon salt
⅛ teaspoon white pepper
⅛ teaspoon ground nutmeg
1 cup popped popcorn
1½ tablespoons butter or margarine
2 tablespoons grated Parmesan cheese
1 teaspoon minced parsley
½ teaspoon dried marjoram leaves
⅛ teaspoon dried chervil leaves

Sauté onion in 2 tablespoons butter in medium saucepan until tender. Stir in carrots, potato, and chicken broth; heat to boiling. Reduce heat and simmer, uncovered, until carrots are tender, about 20 minutes. Process mixture in blender at high speed until smooth. Add cream, yogurt, salt, pepper, and nutmeg; process to blend. To serve hot, return soup to saucepan and heat over medium heat; to serve cold, refrigerate soup until chilled.

Sauté popped corn in 1½ tablespoons butter in large skillet until golden. Sprinkle with cheese, parsley, marjoram, and chervil; toss. Sprinkle over soup before serving. *Makes 4 servings (about 1 cup each).*

Tomato Bisque
with Dill Popcorn Croutons

   1 can (11 ounces) condensed tomato bisque soup
   1 cup milk
   1 teaspoon dry vermouth (optional)
   ½ teaspoon Worcestershire sauce
   ½ cup sour cream or plain yogurt
   1½ tablespoons butter or margarine
   ½ teaspoon dried dillweed
   2 to 4 dashes red pepper sauce
   Pinch dried thyme leaves
   1 cup popped popcorn

Mix tomato bisque soup, milk, vermouth, and Worcestershire sauce in small saucepan; heat just to boiling. Reduce heat to low; stir in sour cream. Cook over low heat until hot through, stirring frequently.

Melt butter in medium skillet; stir in dillweed, red pepper sauce, and thyme. Stir in popped corn; sauté until golden. Sprinkle over soup before serving. *Makes 4 servings (about ⅔ cup each).*

Popcorn in a salad? Of course. The fresh tastes and crisp textures make perfect bowl mates. You can substitute other vegetables in the Garden Salad, although the green pepper, tomato, and avocado share a historical affinity with popcorn—all were unknown to Europeans before Columbus visited America. The Old World may have returned the favor when colonists brought bacon across the ocean and used the drippings to season popcorn—a role they still play in Wilted Spinach and Popcorn Salad. The third salad you'll find here, Tropical Ambrosia, is best suited to dessert time, when it will perk up the appeal of fruit with its topping of caramel corn.

Garden Salad with Popcorn Croutons

       2 cups popped popcorn
       2 tablespoons butter or margarine
       ¼ teaspoon dried basil leaves
       ⅛ teaspoon dried oregano leaves
       ¼ teaspoon garlic powder
       ½ cup vegetable oil
       ¼ cup white wine vinegar
       ¼ teaspoon dried marjoram leaves
       ⅛ teaspoon dried thyme leaves
       ⅛ teaspoon salt
  6 to 8 cups assorted salad greens
       1 tomato, cut into wedges
       1 medium green pepper, cut into strips
       ½ cucumber, scored, sliced
       ½ avocado, peeled, cut into chunks

Sauté popped corn in butter in large skillet until golden; sprinkle with basil, oregano, and garlic powder and toss.

Shake oil, vinegar, marjoram, thyme, and salt in covered jar. Combine greens, tomato, green pepper, cucumber, and avocado in salad bowl; pour dressing over and toss. Sprinkle with popped corn and toss. *Makes 6 servings.*

Wilted Spinach
and Popcorn Salad

    6 cups spinach leaves
    4 ounces fresh mushrooms, sliced
    2 ounces Swiss cheese, cut into strips
    3 hard-cooked eggs, coarsely chopped
    8 slices bacon
    3 green onions and tops, sliced
    ⅓ cup cider vinegar
    1 tablespoon granulated sugar
    2 cups popped popcorn
    1 tablespoon grated Parmesan cheese
       Pepper

Combine spinach leaves, mushrooms, Swiss cheese, and eggs in salad bowl.

Fry bacon in medium skillet until crisp; drain bacon and crumble. Reserve drippings. Sauté onions in 2 tablespoons of the drippings in skillet until tender. Stir in vinegar and sugar; heat to boiling. Reduce heat and simmer 2 minutes. Pour over salad and toss.

Sauté popped corn in 1 tablespoon of the drippings in skillet until golden; sprinkle with Parmesan cheese and toss. Add popped corn to salad and toss. Sprinkle with pepper. *Makes 6 to 8 servings.*

Tropical Ambrosia

    2 cups Island Caramel Corn (see page 39)
    1 can (20 ounces) pineapple chunks, drained
    1 can (16 ounces) peach slices, drained, chopped
    1 cup seedless grapes, cut into halves
    1 large banana, sliced
    1 cup miniature marshmallows
    1 cup whipping cream, whipped
    ⅛ teaspoon ground allspice
    2 dashes ground mace

Make Island Caramel Corn. Combine pineapple, peaches, grapes, banana, and marshmallows in large bowl. Mix whipped cream, allspice, and mace; spoon over fruit mixture and toss. Refrigerate until serving time.

At serving time, sprinkle salad with 1 cup of the caramel corn and toss. Sprinkle remaining caramel corn over top. *Makes 8 servings.*

The surest way to beef up popcorn for family dinners or casual entertaining is by using it to top off hearty Chili Casserole. For chicken, duck, or pork, the appropriate complement is Popcorn and Sausage Stuffing. If you'd like to put popcorn back into Thanksgiving, double the recipe, using a three-quart casserole, and serve it with turkey. Call it culinary justice, if you wish, since the first Thanksgiving is known to have featured popcorn—although the turkey is still in dispute.

Chili Casserole

> 1 **pound ground beef**
> 1 **cup chopped onions**
> 1 **package (1¾ ounces) chili seasoning mix**
> ½ **cup water**
> 1 **can (16 ounces) tomatoes, undrained**
> 2 **cups cooked macaroni**
> 1½ **cups shredded Cheddar cheese**
> 4 **cups popped popcorn**

Cook ground beef in medium skillet until browned; drain fat. Add onions; cook over medium heat 5 minutes. Stir in chili seasoning mix; stir in water, tomatoes and liquid, and macaroni. Heat to boiling. Stir in 1 cup of the cheese. Spoon mixture into greased 2-quart casserole; sprinkle with popped corn and remaining ½ cup cheese. Bake uncovered at 350°F. until hot through, about 20 minutes. *Makes 6 servings.*

Popcorn and Sausage Stuffing

- 5 cups popped popcorn
- 3 cups unseasoned croutons
- 8 ounces pork sausage, cooked, crumbled
- 2 teaspoons dried chives
- ½ teaspoon dried sage leaves
- ¼ teaspoon ground mace
- ⅛ teaspoon pepper
- ¾ cup chicken broth

Combine popped corn, croutons, sausage, chives, sage, mace, and pepper in large bowl; pour broth over and toss. Spoon mixture into greased 1½-quart casserole. Bake covered at 350°F. until hot through, 35 to 40 minutes. Serve with roast chicken, duck, or pork. *Makes 4 servings.*

A most fitting ending to this chapter, Popcorn Indian Pudding updates Native American fare with sugar, spices, and other enrichments. A recipe found in an 1837 midwestern cookbook proved to us that a similar "update" warmed many a cold prairie night long before we discovered it.

Popcorn Indian Pudding

> 6 cups popped popcorn
> ¼ cup cornmeal
> 2 cans (13 ounces each) evaporated milk
> ½ cup packed dark brown sugar
> 2 eggs, beaten
> ½ teaspoon ground cinnamon
> ⅛ teaspoon ground nutmeg
> ⅛ teaspoon ground mace
> 2 tablespoons butter or margarine, softened

Stir popped corn and cornmeal into evaporated milk in large bowl; let stand 4 hours. Stir in sugar and eggs; stir in cinnamon, nutmeg, and mace. Pour mixture into greased 1½-quart casserole; dot top with butter. Place casserole in baking pan, 13" × 9" × 2"; pour 1 inch boiling water into pan. Bake at 300°F. for 1 hour; stir thoroughly. Bake until set, 30 to 40 minutes. Cool until warm. *Makes 6 to 8 servings.*

Note: *Pudding is delicious served warm with scoops of ice cream.*

Chapter 6

Kids Love Popcorn, Too!

If you get a kick out of watching smooth little kernels go wild and crazy when heated, you can appreciate some of the other reasons kids have given for why they love popcorn:

- It sounds good.
- It is the only food that turns inside out when you cook it.
- You know when to stop cooking it because the sound stops.
- You can make it squeak if you chew it the right way.
- You get a lot when you make it.
- Cooks fast. If you don't stop cooking it when the sound stops, it gets burned.
- If your mother eats it all, you can make more.
- Fills you up.
- Looks like you could just dive into it. Looks like snow, only not wet.
- Smells like the movie my brother took me to.
- Cheap. You can afford it.
- Tastes good on the couch with TV.

For kids who like to cook, we offer four additional reasons to love popcorn. Jelly Bean Squares are like a candy. You can make them all by yourself, but you might need someone older to help you pop the corn. All you have to do is mix everything together and press it in a pan (wash your hands, first!). Then you put the pan in the refrigerator and wait—that's the hardest part!

Jelly Bean Squares

> 1 jar (7 ounces) marshmallow cream
> ½ cup peanut butter
> 6 to 8 cups popped popcorn
> 1 cup small jelly beans, assorted flavors

Mix marshmallow cream and peanut butter in large bowl; stir in popped corn and jelly beans until coated evenly. Press mixture into greased 9-inch square baking pan; refrigerate until set, about 4 hours. Cut into squares. *Makes about 1¼ pounds.*

The next two recipes are also very easy. Take out all the ingredients before you start. Measure them with a measuring cup to be sure you have the right amounts. Use a wooden spoon, so that the handle won't get hot, when you are stirring food on the stove.

No-Bake Popcorn Cookies

> 1 package (12 ounces) semisweet chocolate morsels
> 1 package (6 ounces) butterscotch morsels
> ½ cup peanut butter
> 3 cups popped popcorn
> 2 cups honey graham cereal
> 1 cup chow mein noodles

Heat chocolate and butterscotch morsels in large saucepan over low heat until melted, stirring constantly. Stir in peanut butter. Stir in popped corn, graham cereal, and chow mein noodles, stirring to coat evenly. Drop mixture by tablespoonfuls onto wax paper-lined cookie sheets. Refrigerate until firm, about 30 minutes. *Makes about 4 dozen.*

Microwave Method: Microwave chocolate and butterscotch morsels and peanut butter in 3-quart glass casserole at 70% until morsels are melted, 4 to 5 minutes, stirring after 2 minutes. Proceed as above.

Marshmallow Popcorn Squares

¼ cup butter or margarine
4 cups miniature marshmallows
4 to 5 cups popped popcorn
1 cup cocktail peanuts
1 cup miniature chocolate chips

Melt butter in large saucepan; stir in marshmallows. Cook over low heat until melted. Stir in popped corn, peanuts, and chocolate chips; mix to coat evenly. Spread mixture in greased 9-inch square baking pan; refrigerate until set, about 4 hours. Cut into squares. *Makes 2 dozen.*

Microwave Method: Microwave butter and marshmallows in 3-quart glass casserole at High until melted, 2 to 3 minutes; proceed as above.

Easy Caramel Treats are the simplest kind of popcorn ball you can make. They are fun to eat. You can wrap them up in cellophane paper and give them as a gift.
To form the popcorn balls:

- Grease your hands with butter or margarine.
- Let the popcorn mixture cool just until you can touch it.
- Shape the popcorn mixture into balls. Work quickly, or the mixture will get too firm to shape. It is much easier if somebody else works with you.

Easy Caramel Treats

1 bag (1 pound) caramels
¼ cup half-and-half or milk
8 cups popped popcorn
1 cup candy-coated chocolate pieces

Cook caramels and half-and-half in medium saucepan over medium heat until caramels are melted, stirring frequently. Combine popped corn and chocolate pieces in large bowl; pour caramel mixture over and stir to coat evenly. Let cool slightly. Form into small popcorn balls. *Makes about 1 dozen balls.*

> **Microwave Method:** Microwave caramels and half-and-half in 2-quart glass casserole until melted, 4 to 5 minutes, stirring after 2 minutes. Proceed as above.

Parents can delight in the wholesome appetite appeal of popcorn. Dentists and physicians recommend plain popcorn as a substitute for sugary snacks. The following snack mix enhances both the protein content and the crunch of popcorn by combining it with carrot and bologna. Shake it up in a paper bag and the kids can take off with it indoors or out. Accompany the mix with a glassful of the complementary nutrition in Fruit Fizzles, and you can even feature it for lunch.

Bologna and Cheese On the Go

> Vegetable oil
> 1 medium carrot, pared, thinly sliced
> 3 slices bologna, cut into thin strips
> ¼ cup butter or margarine
> 6 cups popped popcorn
> 1½ cups cheese-flavored snack puffs

Heat 1 inch oil in medium saucepan to 375° F.; fry carrot slices in oil until crisp. Drain on paper toweling. Sauté bologna in 2 tablespoons of the butter in small skillet until crisp. Stir in remaining butter until melted. Pour bologna mixture over popped corn in paper bag; shake to mix. Add carrot and cheese-flavored snack puffs; shake to mix. *Makes 4 servings.*

Fruit Fizzles

> 1½ cups chilled orange juice
> ½ cup coarsely chopped fresh or canned peaches

1 tablespoon lemon juice
2 to 3 teaspoons honey
1 egg

Process orange juice, peaches, lemon juice, honey, and egg in blender until foamy; pour into tall glasses. *Makes 2 servings (about 8 ounces each).*

Note: *Pineapple juice can be substituted for the orange juice. Fresh strawberries or banana can be substituted for the peaches.*

A mixture of popcorn and fantasy, Animal Crackers in My Snack will prove an absolute delight at children's parties.

Animal Crackers in My Snack

12 cups popped popcorn
2 boxes (2 ounces each) animal crackers
¾ cup almond brickle chips
2 tablespoons butter or margarine
⅓ cup light corn syrup
¼ cup frozen lemonade concentrate
2 tablespoons honey
1 cup granulated sugar

Combine popped corn, animal crackers, and brickle chips in large bowl. Melt butter in medium saucepan; stir in corn syrup, lemonade concentrate, honey, and sugar. Heat to boiling, stirring constantly, until sugar is dissolved. Reduce heat to low; cook, stirring occasionally, until mixture reaches 250°F. on candy thermometer. Pour syrup mixture over popped corn mixture, stirring to coat evenly. Spread popped corn mixture in jelly roll pan; bake at 250°F. for 45 minutes, stirring every 10 minutes. Cool to room temperature; break into pieces. *Makes about 2 pounds.*

> **Microwave Method:** Microwave butter, corn syrup, lemonade concentrate, honey, and sugar in 2-quart glass casserole at High 2 minutes; stir. Microwave at 70% until mixture reaches 250°F. on candy thermometer, 5 to 6 minutes. Pour syrup mixture over popped corn mixture in 6-quart heatproof bowl. Microwave at High 5 minutes, stirring every minute. Cool in jelly roll pan.

Popcorn Caramel Apples are the kind of homemade treat that can start as an event, become a family ritual—and eventually grow into the warmest memories. They're a natural for Halloween parties and trick-or-treaters.

Popcorn Caramel Apples

> 1 cup whipping cream or half-and-half
> ½ cup dark corn syrup
> ½ cup butter or margarine
> 2 cups packed dark brown sugar
> ¼ teaspoon salt
> 8 medium apples
> 6 cups popped popcorn

Mix cream, corn syrup, butter, sugar, and salt in medium saucepan; heat to boiling, stirring constantly, until sugar is dissolved. Reduce heat to low; cook, without stirring, until mixture reaches 244°F. on candy thermometer.

Insert wooden ice cream sticks in tops of apples; dip apples into caramel mixture, coating evenly. Place on waxed paper-lined cookie sheet or plates. Press popped corn onto caramel mixture. *Makes 8 servings.*

Make popcorn the theme of a children's party, and a world of creativity literally pops open. Highlight the menu with a scrumptious popcorn pizza. The recipe can be doubled or tripled, according to the number of guests. Accompany the pizza with a tossed green salad or fresh vegetable relishes. Then add to the fun by letting each child select favorite flavors for an old-fashioned, ice cream parlor "Cow."

Deep-Pan Popcorn Pizza

- **4** cups popped popcorn
- **1** cup shredded Cheddar cheese
- **1** cup shredded mozzarella cheese
- **½** green pepper, chopped
- **½** cup chopped onion
- **1** tablespoon butter or margarine
- **2** ounces sliced pepperoni, cut into strips
- **½** cup tomato sauce
- **¼** cup sliced pitted ripe olives
- **½** teaspoon dried oregano leaves
- **½** teaspoon dried basil leaves
- **½** teaspoon garlic powder

Spoon 2 cups of the popped corn into bottom of greased 8-inch round cake pan; sprinkle with half the Cheddar and mozzarella cheeses. Sauté green pepper and onion in butter in medium skillet until tender; add pepperoni. Sauté until pepperoni is crisp. Stir in tomato sauce, olives, oregano, basil, and garlic powder; heat to boiling.

Spoon half the sauce mixture over the popped corn in the cake pan; top with remaining popped corn. Spoon remaining sauce mixture over popped corn; top with remaining Cheddar and mozzarella cheeses. Bake at 375°F. for 10 to 12 minutes, until cheese is melted. Cut into wedges. *Makes 4 to 6 servings.*

Fudge Cows

1 can (12 ounces) carbonated fudge soda, chilled
¾ cup vanilla ice cream

Process half the soda and the ice cream in blender until smooth; pour into tall glasses. Slowly pour remaining soda into glasses; serve with straws. *Makes 2 servings (about 8 ounces each).*

Note: *Any desired soda flavor can be used, such as cola, orange, cream, or cherry. Ice cream flavors also can be varied. You might want to try Orange Cows, made with orange soda and orange sherbet.*

After the pizza has been devoured, bring out a tray of frosted cupcakes and put the kids to work "designing" their dessert. Set out popcorn, waxed paper, gumdrops, marshmallows, and assorted small candies. Young guests can flatten the large candies with a rolling pin or soda bottles and cut out shapes with blunt-edged scissors. Then they can decorate the cupcakes with the popcorn and flower shapes inserted on toothpicks. If you wish, you can tint the popcorn by shaking it in a plastic bag with a few drops of food coloring. If the children are too young to shape flowers, you might just give them a supply of popcorn, gumdrops, and jelly beans to press into the cupcake frosting.

Cupcake Flower Garden

1 package (8 ounces) chocolate cake mix
1 can (16.5 ounces) chocolate fudge frosting
3 to 4 cups popped popcorn
Large gumdrops and marshmallows
Small gumdrops, jelly beans, candy decorations

Make cupcakes according to package directions; cool on wire racks. Frost cupcakes with frosting; press popped corn into frosting.

Roll large gumdrops and marshmallows between waxed paper to flatten; cut into circles and decorative shapes for flowers and leaves. Decorate with candy decorations. Fasten flowers and leaves on tops of cupcakes with wooden picks. *Makes 1 dozen cupcakes.*

Here are some other activities that will keep the party popping:

- Make the invitations totally "corny"—with drawings of popcorn characters and an appropriate message. A few possibilities:

- Give the guests sheets of white construction paper and ask them to draw popcorn-character place mats—complete with appropriate facial features and popcorn expressions, of course! Get them started by asking, "What does a popcorn look like?"
- Buy plain, inexpensive paper party hats and let the kids glue on their own popcorn decorations with white household glue. Set out bowls of popcorn tinted several colors.

- Fill a large glass or clear plastic container with popped corn and ask the guests to guess how many kernels.
- Start a popcorn story . . . like the one about the little kernel named Poppy who burst from the corn popper into outer space. . . . Let the kids continue the story until everyone has had a chance—then let each storyteller guess an ending to the tale.
- Older children can see who can write out the most words using only the letters P-O-P-C-O-R-N.
- Pop enough corn to fill a large pillowcase or trash bag. Bury small wrapped prizes or candies in the corn. Then let each child either reach in for a prize or fill a bowl with popcorn to eat on the spot and candies to take home.

Chapter 7

Popcorn Holidays

When crowds gather at Times Square on New Year's Eve to watch a great popcorn ball drop, we'll know that our millennium has arrived. When firecrackers yield to the superior pop of corn—at up to two pounds of force per square inch—we'll celebrate independence twice over. And if people would toss popped corn instead of rice at departing brides and grooms, the honeymoon would start that much sooner.

Lincoln's Birthday is another celebration that should by rights start with corn—to mark the true nourishment of log cabin days. Mardi Gras should bring out the pop-ity-pop of the jazziest sounding refreshment. And what we'd most like to receive on Valentine's Day is five pounds of ribbon-tied popped corn—a twenty-gallon boxful, we calculate, at a quart of kernels per unpopped ounce!

Our ideal valentine would by no means be the first recorded instance of homage paid in popcorn. When Columbus landed in the West Indies, he found the natives selling popcorn decorations like corsages. A sixteenth-century Spanish monk observed that Aztec residents of Mexico draped garlands of popcorn around idols of Tlaloc, the god of fertility and rain. "In similar fashion today," a traveler in 1947 noted, "one may find statues of the Virgin Mary with beautiful necklaces of snowy-white popcorn in little, out-of-the-way chapels in Mexico."

North of the border, at the first Thanksgiving feast (held in 1621), the Iroquois Quadequina, brother of Chief Massasoit, presented the English colonists at Plymouth, Massachusetts, with a deerskin bag filled with several bushels of popped corn.

With Columbus Day (October 12), Mexican Independence Day (September 16), and Thanksgiving clustered on the harvesttime calendar, there's every reason for us to herald the season with popcorn. Harvest Snack Mix will serve all partying purposes; the candies can be omitted if you would prefer an unsweetened snack.

Harvest Snack Mix

2 cups pretzel sticks
1 cup mixed nuts
½ cup sunflower nuts
6 tablespoons butter or margarine
½ teaspoon ground cinnamon
¼ teaspoon ground cloves
8 cups popped popcorn
1 cup candy corn
1 cup chocolate bridge mix

Combine pretzel sticks, mixed nuts, and sunflower nuts in jelly roll pan. Melt butter in small saucepan; stir in cinnamon and cloves. Pour about 2 tablespoons of the butter mixture over pretzel mixture and toss. Pour remaining butter mixture over popped corn in large bowl. Bake pretzel mixture at 300°F. for 30 minutes, stirring in popped corn during last 15 minutes. Cool to room temperature; transfer to large bowl. Add candy corn and bridge mix and toss. *Makes about 12 cups.*

October is National Popcorn month—thirty days of a great excuse for nonstop popping. On the thirty-first day, many popcorn lovers mark the climax of the event by donning scary costumes, smearing their faces with paint, and going to other people's houses to beg for food. We have found that their raucous threats of "Trick or treat!" are best answered with a volley of Orange-Glazed Popcorn. Sometimes we mix black jelly beans with the popped corn, before adding the glaze, just to ward off any evil eye that might be cast by pint-size witches and ghosts.

Orange-Glazed Popcorn

⅔ cup orange juice
2 tablespoons light corn syrup
1¼ cups granulated sugar
Rind of 1 orange, grated
6 cups popped popcorn

Heat orange juice, corn syrup, and sugar to boiling in small saucepan, stirring until sugar is dissolved. Reduce heat to low; cook, stirring occasionally, until mixture reaches 240°F. on candy thermometer. Stir in orange rind. Pour syrup mixture over popped corn in large bowl, stirring to coat evenly. Spread in jelly roll pan; let cool. Break into pieces. *Makes about 1 pound.*

Microwave Method: Microwave orange juice, corn syrup, and sugar in 2-quart glass bowl at High 2 minutes; stir. Microwave at 70% until mixture reaches 240°F. on candy thermometer, 10 to 12 minutes. Proceed as above.

We can recall a time when every fourth November brought popcorn lovers to the forefront of the American political arena. By choosing bags with either Republican or Democratic emblems when they purchased popcorn at the movies, or by mailing in ballots attached to packages of unpopped corn bought at the store, every popcorn consumer could cast a ballot in the National Popcorn Poll. Begun in 1948 by popcorn packer Jim Blevins, the poll accurately predicted the election of presidents Truman (when candidate Thomas Dewey was thought a shoo-in!), Eisenhower, Kennedy, and Johnson before it was discontinued in the late 1960s. Oddly enough, the percentages of total popcorn votes cast for each party came quite close to voting booth tallies, but the Democrats scored much higher than the national norm in movie theaters and the Republicans came out ahead at the supermarket. The reasons for the discrepancy never were explained. However, the Popcorn Poll definitely set a precedent for a popcorn political party—either on election night or during the campaign. Our candidate for a sure victory in November is this apple-and-spice-scented autumn popcorn loaf.

Spiced Popcorn Loaf

> 1 cup apple juice
> 1 teaspoon whole cloves
> 1 teaspoon whole allspice
> 2 cinnamon sticks
> 1¼ cups granulated sugar
> 2 tablespoons light corn syrup
> 8 cups popped popcorn
> 1 cup cashews

Heat apple juice, cloves, allspice, and cinnamon sticks to boiling in small saucepan; reduce heat and simmer 10 minutes. Strain; discard spices. Heat juice mixture, sugar, and corn syrup to boiling in small saucepan, stirring until sugar is dissolved. Reduce heat; cook, stirring occasionally, until mixture reaches 234°F. on candy thermometer. Pour syrup mixture over popped corn and cashews in large bowl, stirring to coat evenly. Press mixture into greased loaf pan, 9″ × 5″ × 4″. Let stand overnight. Remove from pan; cut into slices. *Makes about 1 pound.*

Microwave Method: Microwave apple juice, cloves, allspice, and cinnamon sticks in 2-quart glass casserole at High 5 minutes; strain and discard spices. Return juice mixture to casserole; stir in sugar and corn syrup. Microwave at High 2 minutes; stir. Microwave at 70% until mixture reaches 234°F. on candy thermometer, 10 to 12 minutes. Proceed as above.

December's early days seem endless for those who await Santa's arrival. But for the rest of us, the weeks between Thanksgiving and Christmas fly by all too fast. Popcorn can save many a gift-hunting day in this busy season—and many a dollar, too. Chocolate Popcorn Bark and Popcorn Toffee are easy yet opulent confections to wrap up for Christmas giving. You can store them at room temperature in airtight containers for up to a week. You'll keep them fresher for lucky recipients if you line the gift box or tin with waxed paper and fold it over the candy before securing the lid.

Chocolate Popcorn Bark

3 packages (6 ounces each) semisweet chocolate morsels
2 cups popped popcorn
1 cup unblanched whole almonds

Heat chocolate morsels in medium saucepan over very low heat, stirring constantly, until melted; add popped corn and almonds, stirring to coat evenly. Spread mixture evenly in waxed paper-lined jelly roll pan. Refrigerate until firm, about 30 minutes. Break into pieces. *Makes about 1¼ pounds.*

Microwave Method: Microwave chocolate morsels in 3-quart glass casserole at 70% until melted, 3 to 4 minutes, stirring after 2 minutes. Stir in remaining ingredients; proceed as above.

Popcorn Toffee

1 cup butter or margarine
¼ cup whipping cream or half-and-half
2 cups packed light brown sugar
½ teaspoon vanilla
1 package (6 ounces) semisweet chocolate morsels
2 tablespoons butter or margarine
2 cups popped popcorn

Melt 1 cup butter in medium saucepan; stir in cream, sugar, and vanilla. Heat to boiling, stirring constantly, until sugar is dissolved. Reduce heat to low; cook, stirring occasionally, until mixture reaches 280°F. on candy thermometer. Pour mixture into greased baking pan, 11″ × 7″ × 2″. Let cool until mixture begins to set, about 20 minutes.

Heat chocolate morsels and 2 tablespoons butter in small saucepan over low heat, stirring constantly, until melted. Spread over toffee mixture. Press popped corn into chocolate. Refrigerate until firm, about 30 minutes. Remove from pan; break into pieces with knife. *Makes about 1½ pounds.*

Microwave Method: Microwave 1 cup butter in 2-quart glass casserole at High until melted; stir in cream and sugar. Microwave at 70% until mixture reaches 280°F. on candy thermometer, 10 to 12 minutes. Pour into greased baking pan as above.

Microwave chocolate morsels and 2 tablespoons butter in 2-cup glass measure at 70% until melted, about 2 minutes. Proceed as above.

Because there is a widespread tendency to belittle the significance of popcorn balls, we were delighted to learn that the world's largest popcorn ball—twelve feet in diameter, as measured by the *Guinness Book of World Records*—was conceived and constructed by a professor of culinary arts in 1981 to raise funds for the Peekskill (New York) Area Health Center. Chef Franz Eichenauer stirred together more than 2,000 pounds of corn (donated by a Nebraska grower and popped by the Borden Company), 4,000 pounds of sugar, 280 gallons of corn syrup, and 400 gallons of water. Then he marshaled a team of forty chef-engineers to shape the gooey stuff into blocks, stack the blocks (using forklifts lent by the National Guard), and smooth the outer surface of the sphere with blowtorches. The center of the ball was left hollow and filled with loose popcorn. After the contours of the confection had been duly recorded, an air compressor hooked up to the center of the ball sent the loose popcorn flying in a thirty-foot geyser over the festival site. Fairgoers were covered with delectable "snow"—and all for a very good cause!

Our popcorn ball recipes are much less ambitious in girth. But they come in two irresistible flavors—molasses-walnut and chocolate. Individually wrapped in colored cellophane, they can demonstrate their own fundraising appeal at your favorite organization's next holiday bazaar or bake sale. They also make nice Christmas party souvenirs.

Some cooks claim that it's easier to shape popcorn balls, and

Photograph by Joe Larese/Evening Star

that the results are crunchier, if you keep the popped corn warm in a 250-degree oven until you're ready to pour the syrup over it. In any case, be sure to grease your hands with butter or margarine before you dig into the coated corn. If you enlist someone else to help, you'll stand a better chance of shaping the balls before the syrup cools too much; if the mixture does get too hard to handle, place it in a warm oven for a few minutes. Popcorn-lovers who wish to avoid sticky fingers will appreciate a simple, two-part plastic mold designed solely for shaping popcorn balls. Inexpensive and effective, the popcorn ball maker is distributed by the American Pop Corn Company, makers of Jolly Time popcorn, P.O. Box 178, Sioux City, Iowa 51102.

If you'd rather not spend time forming popcorn balls, you can turn either of these mixtures into a popcorn loaf instead. Press the syrup-coated popped corn into a greased loaf pan, 9" × 5" × 4". Let stand overnight; then remove from pan and cut into slices.

Molasses-Walnut Popcorn Balls

8 cups popped popcorn
1 cup toasted chopped walnuts
1 cup light molasses
½ cup granulated sugar
2 tablespoons butter or margarine

Combine popped corn and walnuts in large bowl. Heat molasses, sugar, and butter to boiling in small saucepan, stirring until sugar is dissolved. Reduce heat to low; cook, stirring occasionally, until mixture reaches 250°F. on candy thermometer. Pour syrup mixture over popped corn mixture; form into popcorn balls. *Makes about 1 dozen.*

Microwave Method: Microwave molasses, sugar, and butter in 2-quart glass bowl at High 2 minutes; stir. Microwave at 70% until mixture reaches 250°F. on candy thermometer, 5 to 6 minutes. Proceed as above.

Chocolate Popcorn Balls

½ cup water
¼ cup corn syrup

1 **cup granulated sugar**
1 **cup semisweet chocolate morsels**
8 **cups popped popcorn**

Combine water, corn syrup, sugar, and chocolate morsels in small saucepan. Cook over medium heat, stirring frequently, until chocolate is melted and sugar is dissolved. Cook over medium-high heat, stirring occasionally, until mixture reaches 250°F. on candy thermometer. Pour syrup mixture over popped corn in large bowl, stirring to coat evenly. Form into popcorn balls. *Makes about 1 dozen.*

Microwave Method: Microwave water, corn syrup, sugar, and chocolate morsels in 2-quart glass casserole at High 4 minutes, stirring after 2 minutes. Microwave at 70% until mixture reaches 250°F. on candy thermometer, about 15 minutes. Proceed as above.

To our eyes, there is no tree ornament more graceful than simple strands of popcorn, with or without cranberries interspersed. But since the truly creative popper refuses to stop until all possibilities have been tested—and consumed!—we've lately taken to playing with sculpted popcorn ornaments. You'll find general directions and shaping suggestions on the next page. The Pomander Popcorn Balls mingle a wonderful fragrance with that of the evergreen boughs. The Cinnamon Popcorn Balls add flecks of cheery red color. As for the more elaborate shapes, we did manage a recognizable gingerbread man, and the candy canes are unmistakable, but when someone thought our angels were white butterflies, well, we just took it as flattery! Artistic friends of ours go in for free-form popcorn baubles and freestanding edifices, like snowmen and large wreaths. They say the shaping potential is infinite. So far, we've proved only that you can eat every morsel you make.

Two touches of artistry are easily mastered. First, you can tint the syrup any color you want with a few drops of food coloring. And secondly, if you press an ice cream stick into any portion of this mixture, some child will gladly accept it as a lollipop masterpiece.

Grease your hands with butter or margarine before sculpting and refer to the hints for making popcorn balls if the mixture should cool too much before your reindeer landscape is complete. If you'd prefer to stick to old-fashioned popcorn garlands, let the popped corn stand overnight for easier stringing and use nylon thread or dental floss. And while you're planning ornaments, do remember the birds of winter with some outdoor strands of popcorn and suet.

Holiday Popcorn Decorations

¾ cup light corn syrup
¼ cup water
1 teaspoon distilled white vinegar
2 tablespoons butter or margarine
1 cup granulated sugar
10 cups popped popcorn

Heat corn syrup, water, vinegar, butter, and sugar to boiling in medium saucepan, stirring until sugar is dissolved. Reduce heat to low; cook, stirring occasionally, until mixture reaches 250°F. on candy thermometer. Pour syrup mixture over popped corn in large bowl, stirring to coat evenly. Shape and decorate popped corn mixture, using the following variations.

Pomander Popcorn Balls: Make syrup mixture as above, adding 2 tablespoons grated orange rind to mixture. Form popped corn mixture into small balls. Press whole cloves into popcorn balls. Press Christmas tree hooks into tops of balls, if desired. Let stand until hardened. *Makes 1 dozen.*

Chocolate Dipped Popcorn Balls: Form popped corn mixture into small balls; let cool. Press Christmas tree hooks into tops of balls, if desired. Melt 1 package (12 ounces) semisweet chocolate morsels in small saucepan over low heat; stir in 3 to 4 tablespoons softened butter or margarine for desired dipping consistency. Dip 1 side of each popcorn ball into chocolate; refrigerate until chocolate is firm, about 15 minutes. *Makes 1 dozen.*

Cinnamon Popcorn Balls: Make syrup mixture as above, adding ¼ cup red cinnamon candies to mixture. Form popped corn mixture into balls; press Christmas tree hooks into tops of balls, if desired. *Makes 1 dozen.*

Christmas Ornament Shapes: Form popped corn mixture into candy canes, tree shapes, angels, gingerbread men, or other desired Christmas shapes. Decorate with assorted candies. Press Christmas tree hooks into tops of shapes, if desired. *Makes about 1 dozen.*

Microwave Method: Microwave corn syrup, water, vinegar, butter, and sugar in 2-quart glass casserole at High 4 minutes, stirring after 2 minutes. Microwave at 70% until mixture reaches 250°F. on candy thermometer, 5 to 6 minutes. Proceed as above.

A Styrofoam cone simplifies the sculpting of a foot-high Christmas centerpiece. Assemble ribbon or yarn bows, small pinecones, beads, tinsel, shells, candies, or whatever trimmings you'd like before you start cooking. Then you'll be ready to press all decorations into the corn right away. Tint the syrup green with food coloring, if you wish. If you have a large cone, you can shape a taller tree from a double batch of the corn mixture.

Christmas Tree Centerpiece

> 1 cup light corn syrup
> ¼ cup water
> 1 teaspoon distilled white vinegar
> 2 tablespoons butter or margarine
> 1 cup packed light brown sugar
> 10 cups popped popcorn
> Assorted candies, string licorice, holly, ribbon, etc.

Heat corn syrup, water, vinegar, butter, and sugar to boiling in medium saucepan, stirring until sugar is dissolved. Reduce heat to low; cook, stirring occasionally, until mixture reaches 250°F. on candy thermometer. Pour syrup mixture over popped corn in large bowl, stirring to coat evenly. Let cool until warm. Press popped corn mixture onto 12-inch Styrofoam cone. Decorate as desired with candy, holly, and ribbon. *Makes 1 tree.*

It's neither fun nor fair-minded for one person to attempt all popcorn trimmings by himself. And as soon as you get a second person involved, you have the nucleus of a popcorn party. So then you need to have on hand some Yuletide-spirited snack— such as this easy-to-make, cherry-brightened indulgence.

Tree-Trimmers' Popcorn

> 8 cups popped popcorn
> 1 cup macadamia nuts
> 1 cup flaked coconut
> ½ cup maraschino cherries, well drained, cut into halves
> ¼ cup butter or margarine
> 2 tablespoons pineapple preserves
> 2 tablespoons light brown sugar

Combine popped corn, macadamia nuts, coconut, and cherries in large bowl. Heat butter, preserves, and sugar in small saucepan until mixture is boiling and sugar is dissolved. Pour butter mixture over popped corn mixture and toss. Spread popped corn mixture in jelly roll pan; bake at 300°F. for 30 minutes. *Makes about 8 cups.*

Note: *Any kind of nuts can be substituted for the macadamia nuts.*

Microwave Method: Microwave butter, preserves, and sugar in 6-quart glass bowl at High 2 minutes. Stir in remaining ingredients; microwave at High until crisp, 5 to 6 minutes, stirring every minute.

For children the popcorn pièce de résistance at holiday time is likely to be a Popcorn Candy House. Much easier to construct than a gingerbread house, it invites the same play of imagination—Mr. and Mrs. S. Claus, Hansel and Gretel, or Snow White and the Seven Dwarfs would all feel right at home here. Once you've put the house together and covered it with frosting, children of any age can apply the popcorn and decorations. They will probably find it easier to wield a tube of frosting than a pastry bag to outline the windows and doors.

Popcorn Candy House

2 packages (7.2 ounces each) fluffy white frosting
   mix
1 cup powdered sugar
8 cups popped popcorn
½ cup melted butter or margarine
1 package (3 ounces) strawberry flavor gelatin
1 package (3 ounces) lime flavor gelatin
Assorted candies
1 cup canned or homemade chocolate buttercream
   frosting

Construct house, using lightweight cardboard or poster board, following diagrams for size and shape; attach pieces with masking tape.

Make frosting mix according to package directions, beating in powdered sugar. Toss popped corn with melted butter; divide corn into two bowls. Sprinkle strawberry gelatin over popped corn in 1 bowl; sprinkle lime gelatin over popped corn in second bowl. Toss popped corn to coat evenly.

Frost sides and roof of house with fluffy frosting. Press colored popped corn and candies onto frosting to decorate house. To make windows and doors, pipe buttercream frosting through pastry tube with medium writing tip. *Makes 1 house.*

Note: *Any flavor gelatin can be used, depending on colors desired. You may wish to purchase a tube of decorating frosting to use instead of the buttercream frosting and pastry tube.*

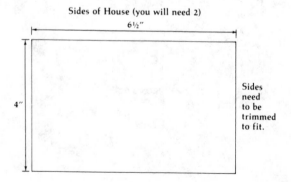

Sides of House (you will need 2)

6½"

4"

Sides
need
to be
trimmed
to fit.

Roof (you will need 2)

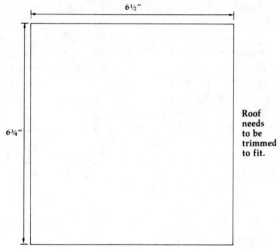

6½″

6¾″

Roof needs to be trimmed to fit.

Front and Back of House (you will need 2)

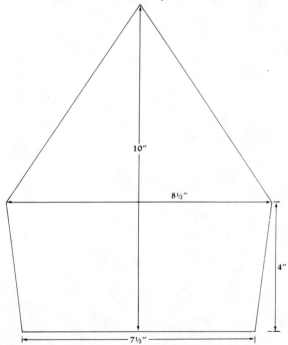

10″

8½″

4″

7½″

And one popcorn PS for the holidays: Popcorn will insulate and protect fragile gifts ranging from glassware to cookies. Line the gift box with a plastic bag for neatest unwrapping and layer the popcorn around the objects to be sent. Corn popped without oil is often preferred, but popped-in-oil corn will work fine if the package isn't going to sit around for months. One advantage popcorn has over plastic foam cushioners is natural recycling: even if the corn is too stale to eat, the recipient can toss it outside for the birds—who will love your gift, too. Commercial shippers have reported that popcorn offers better protection against breakage than excelsior—the proof being a popcorn-packed lamp dropped from a one-story height by a manufacturer in Flushing, Queens, and retrieved without a scratch.

Chapter 8

Popcorn Memorabilia

We collect nothing but popcorn memories. All the rest gets eaten. But you might be interested in other rites that have developed around the art of popping corn.

In Marion, Ohio, not far from Columbus and close to where the corn grows, there's a destination worthy of all popcorn-loving pilgrims. Called the Wyandot Popcorn Museum, it is a tribute both to late nineteenth- and early twentieth-century inventors and manufacturers of mechanical popping equipment and to the thousands of individual vendors who used to sell popcorn from sidewalk wagons and candy store counters. George K. Brown, president of the Wyandot Popcorn Company and premier historian of the popcorn industry, collected and supervised restoration of the antique poppers. Located at 135 Wyandot Avenue in Marion, the museum is open Tuesday through Saturday (Sunday also from May 1 to September 30) from noon to 6:00 p.m. Admission is free.

Inside the museum, you'll be reminded why popcorn was not a booming business prior to around 1890. An example of a hand sheller—a multitoothed, cast-iron model operated with an aching amount of muscle power—hangs in one corner. Across the room, there's a giant-sized, long-handled basket suspended over

"1899 No. 1 Cretors Popcorn Wagon." Originally sold for $400 to Mr. Hill of Decatur, Illinois in Feb. 1899. Third oldest surviving Cretors Wagon.

an old-fashioned candy stove—a souvenir of somebody's steadfast agitation. Arrayed between these artifacts are the steampowered machines that ushered in the golden age of popcorn, including a model produced by Charles Cretors in 1899. Glorious, indeed, are the hand-carved woodwork, beveled-glass windows, and nickel-plated copper fittings of the old Cretors wagons. Come to the museum and you'll realize what respect for popcorn once meant!

Behind every one of those beautiful old wagons lies a story of popcorn survival—and much more than survival for some lucky, hard-working souls. The archives of C. Cretors and Company, which still makes commercial popping equipment in its Chicago plant, hold hundreds of these stories. They detail, in one way or another, the benefits derived from buying a machine and going into the popcorn business. The following letter, written by A. C. Primm of Lodi, California, and dated October 27, 1912, is typical:

> ... I started business here June 26th with a No. 1 Wagon, Model A, and am surprised at the amount of business I have done, this being a town of 3,500 people. I am always ready to meet my payments as they come due, have kept a family of five, paid house rent and city license and save from $20 to $25 per month. I have never been able to find any other business where I could do this with such a small outlay of cash to begin with. My advice to anyone who has saved a few hundred dollars and is tired of working for the "other fellow" is buy a Cretors Machine, get in a good town and begin working for yourself.

The spirit of popcorn entrepreneurship, if not the steam-powered equipment, flourishes even today. You'll find two shrines of the art in New York City. At Popcorn Paradise, on Thirty-fourth Street, the popcorn is colored every hue from green to lavender—reflecting a choice of thirty flavors that includes butter rum and "ball park hot dog." At actor Jack Klugman's popcorn show on Fifty-ninth Street, called Jack's Corn Crib, the twenty-eight seasoning specials range from pizza to piña colada.

Closer to the heart of corn-growing country, in the land that stretches from Ohio to Nebraska, you can participate in the late-summer popcorn festivals and fairs held in Ridgway, Illinois; Valparaiso, Indiana; Van Buren, Indiana; Hamburg, Iowa; Schaller, Iowa; Ord, Nebraska; and Marion, Ohio. All of these towns are centers of popcorn production; the activities in Marion and Valparaiso attract the largest crowds. Write to the local chamber of commerce for precise dates, if you wish to attend.

Many popcorn lovers scour corn country in search of antique popcorn paraphernalia, which has gained greatly in value with age. Some even collect a variety of pressed glassware called "popcorn glass." Made by glass companies in Pennsylvania and Ohio from the late 1860s to the late 1880s, these bowls, pitchers, and such feature a motif of pointed "kernels" separated by stippled ornaments that resemble ears of corn. People who knit and crochet continue, as generations have, to work clusters of "popcorn stitches" into sweaters and afghans. You'll find all of these diversions detailed in antiques and crafts publications—strong testimony to popcorn's secure place in the heart of Americana.

Index